WAR, PEACE AND THE DERRY JOURNAL

Layout/design by Neil Roddy - www.fudgedesigns.co.uk
Printed by Bizzprint

First published November 2023.
Colmcille Press, Ráth Mór Centre, Derry BT48 0LZ
Managing Editor Garbhán Downey
www.colmcillepress.com

Colmcille Press gratefully acknowledges the support of Creggan Enterprises Limited and the John Bryson Foundation.

The John Bryson Foundation

ISBN 978-1-914009-38-9
A CIP copy for this book is available from the British Library.

CONTENTS

Acknowledgements

I retired as Managing Editor of Derry Journal Group Newspapers in 2006. That was my job title then. I had overall editorial responsibility for the Group's seven titles.

As I said, that was my "responsibility", but in my eyes my real job was editing the Derry Journal. It was a job I loved.

The Journal is one of the oldest papers in the world, and back in the day it punched way above its weight. With local players like John Hume, Martin McGuinness, Bishop Edward Daly, Brian Friel, Seamus Heaney et al, it had real status and massive influence. To me being editor in that time and in that place was a privilege, by far the thing I am most proud of in my career.

As you will read in this book, the 25 years I was to spend in the Editor's Chair on the Buncrana Road was to prove a real roller-coaster. It was far from easy, and there were some very tough days.

But along the way I met some great people who helped smooth my path.
Firstly, I have to pay tribute to Journal proprietor, F.E. McCarroll for giving me the job, and to his son Colm for convincing his dad to take the risk, a big risk, in entrusting his precious newspaper over to a 28-year-old, wet-behind-the-ears Donegal man. I owe them.

I hope I repaid their faith in the years that followed.

People will fall through the cracks of my memory - and I apologise here and now for that - but colleagues like Liam McCandless, Billy McLaughlin, Joe Martin, John McManus are unforgettable. They went out of their way to help me find my feet in those turbulent early days. Sadly quite a few of the old hands have now passed on. I frequently think of them.

Honourable mentions to some great editorial colleagues are to be found in the book. So, read on. To them I am eternally grateful as without them, I would have floundered. I was always good at picking brains, and thank God there were plenty of good brains to pick.

To the Journal itself, I would like to acknowledge the massive force for good it has been in my life and offer a major hat-tip to my former colleagues Sean McLaughlin and Michael Wilson who remain resolutely in that worthy newsroom, keeping the candle lit. And it's great to see Jim McCafferty, once a stalwart of the production and editorial departments, still showing his talent in the Journal pages as a photographer.

The first person who suggested I write my memoirs was an old friend, Fr. Kevin O'Doherty, the parish priest of Newtowncunnigham. I met him for a coffee not too long after my retirement and his advice was "write it down now while it's all fresh in your memory." It was great advice. I started the next week.

Unfortunately, that was followed by a 12-year hiatus where I didn't write a word. But I thank him for planting the seed and, later, Garbhán Downey for getting my nose back to the grindstone. We all need the proverbial kick in the rear-end now and then. Thanks also to the team at Colmcille Press - Neil Roddy, Joe Martin, Conal McFeely, Úna McNally and Jacqui Begley - for bringing this all into being with such great care.

I would also pay tribute to my late mother and father, Cassie and Pat - they were the salt of the earth - and my brothers and sisters for the great joy in having a supportive family. It's been a blessing.

Finally, there is one person who was with me the day I started my first job way back in 1974 and was still there when I, finally, wrapped it all up in 2014 and that is my wife, Rosie. She was there in the good times and the bad times. She took a lot of flak on occasions simply for being the wife of the Editor of the Derry Journal, but not once did she ever complain or let me down. For that I owe her and my three sons - Shane, Aaron and Paddy - everything.
I am not abashed to say they, literally, mean the world to me.

FOREWORD
By Garbhán Downey

For twenty-five years, as editor of the largest newspaper group in the North West, Pat McArt knew and understood more about what was happening in Derry than anyone. All the region's different siloes – military and paramilitary, social, economic, legal, cultural and clerical – fed into the Journal. And while they might not have been speaking to one another, they all spoke to the Journal and, for the most part, trusted it.

The paper was, to paraphrase Arthur Miller, the essence of a small nation talking to itself. In the years before social media, the Journal was an unmissable part of civic life, going into every single home in the North West every Tuesday and Friday, the centre of every conversation.

If Hume was Derry's brain, McGuinness its eyes and ears, and Daly its conscience, McArt - and the Journal - was its beating heart. And, of course, its voice.

The Journal was integral to society because, quite simply, it was society. Its influence as both a paper of record and a shaper of opinion was almost absolute, in a way that those born since the demise of regional newspapers and local radio could never possibly comprehend. From pigeon-racing to politics, there wasn't a feather that got ruffled without the Journal having something to say about it.

At the centre of the maelstrom stood McArt, a Donegal blow-in, whose colourful language and self-puncturing humour belied a profound intellect and a calm determination to pursue positive change for his adopted city. His outsider's eye, which gave him the ability to see over the parish wall into the wider world, coupled with his particular understanding of how our Southern neighbours thought and acted, brought an even-tempered, outward-looking sense of perspective to the Journal, in the midst of what had become a bad-tempered, inward-looking war.

McArt's book, as he repeatedly makes clear, is neither a history nor a biography. It is, rather, a memoir; a personal story replete with personal reflections. In saying that, it will be read for generations to come as, perhaps, the definitive account of the monumental changes that were taking place in Derry in the latter part of the 20th century.

In 1995, in the midst of the marching disputes, the banner headline on the Journal's front page once proclaimed 'Eyes of the World are on Derry'. And it was no idle boast. What Derry did was important, and what the paper said counted. The main players were based here, and the private negotiations, which ultimately settled the 800-year conflict between Britain and Ireland, took place within a mile of the Journal office.

So, just as *Derry, Countdown to Disaster,* written by McArt's predecessor Frank Curran, has become the go-to handbook for students of the civil rights era, this memoir will rapidly become the number one pick for students of the subsequent conflict and the peace process.

As a boss, McArt was a strong leader, who inspired confidence in his staff. He always stood up for his women and men, no matter how tricky or high-ranking the opponent. But, if necessary, he was affable and diplomatic enough to trim your sails and rechart your course without it becoming an issue.

He was fair and open-minded, rarely if ever held agendas, and was a master at handling the many monster egos that crossed the Journal threshold. He worked on the theory that an editor's job was not to be the smartest person in the room but was to work out whomever might be the smartest person in the room at any given moment – and to listen to that person. And yet for all that, McArt was, himself, very often the smartest person in any room he went into, not that he would ever let on.

If anything, in the pages that follow, McArt underestimates his own importance as a player and minimises his role in the changes that took place in Derry under his watch. Yet for decades, on behalf of the people of Derry and the wider North, he acted both as our advisor to, and chief scrutineer of, the Irish, British and US governments. He also served, privately and publicly, as the trusted critic and counsellor of all our local giants, improving and challenging them – and more often than not leading and directing them. It is important to remember that this was an era when, as far as all these individuals and groups were concerned, the Journal was the final arbiter and the ultimate authority.

McArt's modesty aside, and his is the genuine sort - he never worried about what others were saying and continued wearing the sweater-vests - this book is riveting. It is insightful, serious and meaningful, but can also be funny and irreverent. After all, this is the man who in the midst of some of Derry's darkest days gave birth to the long-running, satirical JED column, which reminded the city it was okay to laugh again.

No. This book is not a history and it is not a biography. But if you want to acquire a true impression of what happened in northwest Ireland between the nadir of the Troubles and the beginning of the new peace, there is no better starting point.

Pat McArt has been telling stories all his life and this one is undoubtedly the greatest of them all.

PROLOGUE

You cannot be serious?!

According to the records, such as they are, in the 250 years of its existence I was one of the longest-serving editors of the Derry Journal. Possibly even the longest. As longevity in the media industry is not to be sneezed at, I would like to get that on the record that I was in the Editor's Chair for the best part of a quarter of century.

In 1981 I left 'a good job' – my mother's description – as a journalist and sub-editor with RTE in Dublin and came to Derry. When I told her of my decision her response was a straight lift from the tennis player, John McEnroe: 'You cannot be serious?!' She had a point.

I am not exaggerating when I say it was a culture shock of considerable magnitude hitting Derry in the early 1980s. You leave a city such as Dublin where people went out to work, out to the pub at night and there was normality. By complete contrast, the atmosphere in Derry was so febrile the old cliché 'you could cut the tension with a knife' was almost a factual reality.

My timing was very telling. Just a few months prior to my arrival two young local men, Patsy O'Hara and Mickey Devine, had died on hunger strike in Long Kesh, and amidst the sorrow and mourning there was an undercurrent of seething rage. It was palpable.

I can recall vividly that first day in Derry. Black flags were flying from just about every window in the huge housing estates in Creggan, Shantallow and the Bogside, and as far as I could tell there was pro-hunger strike graffiti on just about every strategically-located gable wall. It was ubiquitous. Heavily-armoured British army jeeps were everywhere. They all had a soldier with a semi-automatic machine gun popping out of a hole cut in the roof. This guy's designated role was to prevent attacks by frequently cocking an eye into his gunsight to scan passing pedestrians as they travelled along.

Unlike the Gardaí, the police force, the RUC, was armed, and they didn't walk around the streets – they, like the Brits, travelled in convoy using the same type of heavy-duty vehicles. There was no stopping for chats or friendly banter as I had seen police in my hometown engage in.

It hit me particularly strongly what I had got myself into when I drove along and noted not a single street light remained on the main thoroughfare of

Strand Road. The IRA, I was told, had shot them all out so as to provide ease of movement for their Active Service Units during hours of darkness

To be leaving a well-paid job with the national broadcaster and joining a paper in a place of civil unrest, a city clearly in turmoil with violence a regular occurrence, does seem, in retrospect, an odd decision; my mother, as already mentioned, was not alone in expressing the opinion that my decision bordered on some kind of nihilism.

I was, most definitely, leaving a good job in RTE. Indeed, just weeks before I had been offered the prospect of promotion to senior sub-editor, where the salary was good and where a climb up the greasy pole to management was a real possibility. To be moving to Derry with that kind of opportunity staring me in the face didn't make a lot of sense.

But it was never, for me, about money or prospects. It was something more visceral than that. Growing up in Letterkenny, Derry – and what was happening there – was a magnet.

Just twenty miles up the road from where I lived there were events occurring that were making headlines across the globe. Night after night in our house we sat glued to the television switching from RTE to UTV to BBC to catch the big debates where gladiators like Paisley, Hume, Captain Terence O'Neill et al came on air each evening to do battle for their tribe. This was drama, this was tragedy, this was life on the edge. Any newsperson worth his/her salt would have been intrigued by it all, and I certainly was. This was drama on steroids.

For me the thought of being Editor of an historic and respected newspaper like the Journal, which was positioned front and centre of this conflict, was a real draw. With that too came the prospect of being a big fish in a small pond instead of a small fish in a big pond. That, to my mind at the time, was not to be sneezed at either. I don't really know why.

Anyway, I made my decision and I have no regrets.

Many major historic events were to happen in the years that were to follow that decision and I had a ringside seat for quite a few; sometimes, I even made it into the ring myself..

In 2006 I called it a day. I can honestly say the changes between the day I started and the day I finished are so, so numerous as to be almost surreal. It's hard to believe that it's the same place – Derry today is a city almost 180 degrees different from the one I arrived in.

This is my version of those years. At the outset, I would like to make it clear that this is not a history of any kind. What I have written is my version of events as I understood them. They are subjective opinions and are open to challenge, so I'll leave the factual, academic version of history to others.

Secondly, this is a memoir not an autobiography.

I never kept a diary and I decided against doing voluminous research on the somewhat facile basis that if I couldn't remember it off the top of my head it was hardly worth writing about.

It's a memoir in the sense that it's about various events and people, and most chapters could be read as stand-alone stories. And while Derry takes centre stage for much of it, there are other tales about the people, places and events I encountered along the way, of the things that impacted on my life and shaped me – for good or ill.

Finally, many people played a role in being catalysts for this book but none more than my former colleague Garbhán Downey who told me one day as we were having egg and chips in a café on the Border to 'write it all down before you get Alzheimer's'.

As publishers go, that really was subtle motivation.

So, keeping that in mind, here goes....

LET'S BEGIN AT THE END

It is a strange way to tell a story but let me start by telling of my last day at the Derry Journal. It was a bitingly cold, gun-metal grey kind of day, a Monday afternoon at the end of February 2014, when I walked out the door for the last time. Clichéd as it sounds, the weather matched my mood.

I had made the decision earlier that I would leave quietly, so I slipped out on the pretext I was off to get a cup of coffee from the wee huckster shop across the road and I didn't come back. I didn't need the fuss of another 'leaving do'– photographs, speeches, long goodbyes. I already had all those years earlier – back in 2006 – when I had retired as Managing Editor.

This time I was leaving a part-time position because redundancies were coming down the track. From my own experience in management I knew how bean counters worked so I was certain I was in their crosshairs. They would have made the calculation I was getting paid too much for contributing too little; that would be debatable, but the fact was incontrovertible that as I was only working three days a week and getting paid like a full-time member of staff I could see how they would look at it.

From reading the room when management had talks with staff some time earlier about the need for ever increasing cutbacks, I had no doubts whatsoever that my thirty-two-year connection with the Journal was coming to an end. So, I had made the decision for both myself and the bosses by applying for 'voluntary' redundancy which had been accepted.

Now that final day had arrived, the atmospherics were straight out of Hollywood central casting. Against the biting wind I started walking. I was, now that I think about it, almost in a daze. Just a few hundred yards from the Journal's brand spanking new hi-tech offices at Duncreggan Road I soon passed the old Journal building on the Buncrana Road where I had spent my entire career as Editor. I instinctively stopped. I knew this was important to me psychologically, that I needed to take cognisance that something that had been a major part of my life was over.

As I gazed at that old building, now isolated and in total darkness, I found it all but impossible to believe it was being used as a storeroom for a supermarket. To me it was a kind of sacrilege. The times, the craic, the memories we all had of that place made it almost sacred to me.

The mind is a strange thing in that I knew instinctively I needed to take stock, to rationalise what was happening as I faced into a very different future. Standing there I remembered the many times the icon that was John Hume had come down and outlined what was happening politically. Many were the rows we had too in my office. A political giant, and a man with a brain the size of a planet, 'Saint John' could, I often found, be a difficult person to deal with if you diverged from his viewpoint.

I had a flashback too to the day I got into an argument with IRA leader, Martin McGuinness and told him to fuck off.

It was a huge day for Derry when Garret FitzGerald became the first serving Taoiseach to visit the city, and he brought a huge entourage to the 'Journal' - we were the centerpiece of the visit – in the mid-1980s. Politically, that was a real big deal, significant in that it told us that change was, finally, in the air, that Dublin was getting a role in Northern affairs.

Those passing by that winter's day in 2014, hurrying to get bread, milk and toilet rolls in the supermarket that now fronted the old Journal building, would have found it all-but-impossible to believe that it had once been the fulcrum of the biggest news-gathering operation in the North-West, that it housed the busiest provincial editorial newsroom in the country.

Deserted and in darkness now, it was often like Piccadilly Circus back in the day.

What was going through my head was a kind of outlier thought that most people in the city weren't aware of, the fact that despite the Troubles and the danger, British army officers used to call in regularly to that building. In the main they wanted to have a chat about how the nationalist people were feeling, and to see if they could improve their image and/or reputation with the local populace. God bless their little cotton socks as I had to tell more than one naïve officer that, after Bloody Sunday, lifting water with a net would have been easier than improving their PR.

It's a ridiculous thing to have to admit now but, as the troubles had ensured tourists were few, a non-Derry accent in those days was an absolute rarity - so having these guys with their upper crust accents in the office always added a bit of colour to an otherwise run-of-the-mill groundhog-type day. It was so unusual.

Away from all that, I recalled too a person who I can only describe as deranged standing outside my window, mouth frothing in his rage yelling 'I am going to fucking kill you'. He had wanted some hare-brained article published, and after many subtle attempts to let him down gently, to tell him it wouldn't be happening, I had to take a stronger line when asking him to get out of the office. He then went totally ape.

Another of this ilk landed late one night off his head on something I suspect was much stronger than alcohol, threatening similar retribution if a story about his son appeared. With the help of a couple of colleagues I physically removed him. I didn't take him seriously though. I should have, as last I heard, he was actually serving time for murder.

And, of course, there were the inimitable members of staff. God, what an array of brilliant characters.

Amongst these were Domhnall MacDermott who, tragically, died in his 30s. He was a true intellectual, enjoyed a very hectic social life but never missed a day at work. He had such good contacts in the Republican Movement, he got more important stories during the Troubles than any reporter in the country.

And then there was Siobhan McEleney, a lovely woman, devoted mother of four wee girls, who was the Deputy Editor for many years. Siobhan died of a brain tumour in her 40s. She was a one-off, irreplaceable. She often comes into my mind to this day. Most people in the North-west will still remember Larry Doherty, the chief photographer who, thanks to the Troubles, his hard-working, fearless nature, and the massive global demand for photographs of the conflict, could afford a house on the Culmore Road and a boat on the Swilly.

One story Larry delighted in telling was how he was out one day when he came across an army patrol and suddenly a small, terrier-type dog bolted out of nowhere and grabbed the trouser leg of a passing soldier. Larry, quick as a flash, got out his camera, snapped it, and then got paid a fortune – I recall 600 dollars being mentioned – by an American magazine which put it on the cover. 600 dollars could have bought a very good second-hand car back then

This additional income stream gave him the kind of lifestyle few other photographers in local media these days would ever be able to attain. He could, on occasions, be a torture, but what a character!

One of the strangest phone calls of my life was in late May 1991. It is never good when your phone rings loudly in your hall in the middle of the night. My wife went down to answer it and came back up to tell me that one of our reporters, Mark McFadden, was on the phone and wanted to talk to me urgently. I went down and Mark told me that a Donegal County Councillor, Sinn Fein's Eddie Fullerton, had just been assassinated by loyalists in his home in Buncrana. This marked a massive escalation of the Troubles, the first time loyalists had crossed the Border to murder an Irish public representative.

It never even occurred to me to ask Mark how he had got the news so quickly.

I could go on and on and on about these great people and so, so many others. I would contend Derry made and shaped them to be the people they were. I am absolutely certain we will not see their likes again.

All that and more hit me that day.

Most people have heard the old saying that when you are dying your life flashes before you. That day standing in the howling wind outside that now lifeless building I was given a sort of premature version of that. It might sound more than a bit on the dramatic side to suggest this but I had lived a sort of vicarious life few journalists got to experience, dealing with events and people where it was often, quite literally a matter of life and death. And I wasn't always a spectator on the side lines, I was centre stage for so much of it. Now it was all over.

My life, I knew, would never be the same again.

DERRY ON THE WORLD STAGE

Coming to Derry shouldn't really have been an odd thing to do as the Journal had a magnetic attraction for me. And as that is a strange thing to say, I should provide some context.

I don't recall who first stated it, though something tells me it might have been the afore-mentioned Larry Doherty. I had met him at a function in Donegal years earlier and we had had a conversation about life in Derry in general, and about the Journal in particular.

Whether or not it was Larry, I clearly remember being told that in Derry there were only three positions which really counted - the MP, the Catholic Bishop, and the Editor of the Derry Journal. These, I was given to understand, were the three people of status who had most influence in the community.

I was but a callow youth when I heard that, but it was to prove a significant harbinger of the life that was to come my way. Anyway, as the MP was John Hume and the Catholic Bishop was Dr. Edward Daly, for two of three that claim of local gravitas was certainly true. They were major figures not just locally but nationally and internationally.

It's almost akin to stating it snows in the Arctic in winter when explaining that Hume was then easily the most famous political leader on the island of Ireland, a heavyweight player on the world stage, a man who could lift a phone and get directly through to presidents and prime ministers across the globe. I was, eventually, to see first-hand him do that regularly - but I am getting ahead of myself here. I didn't know that then.

Eddie Daly too was an iconic figure, the priest seen waving a white handkerchief as a group of men carry the dying 17-year-old Jackie Duddy, the first shooting victim of Britain's Parachute Regiment on that infamous day in January 1972, the day which was to become known as Bloody Sunday.

For a time that photograph had the same global recognition as the famed poster of Che Guevara. It had catapulted Daly into the media spotlight and for years after he was a regular on media in the States, in Britain and across Europe.

So, it doesn't take Sherlock Holmes to deduce these were serious people in a serious place at a really serious point in time. What I had never anticipated was that one day I would be the third leg of that particular stool.

The reality is that I was, on appointment, a 28-year-old, politically wet-behind-the-ears Donegal man, who was hardly a household name in his own house, never mind out in the big bad world. And as I wasn't brought up in the city, had never lived there, had hardly even visited the place, I could see why some folks saw it as a very strange appointment.

While I had edited the paper on several occasions in the short few months I was there when the then Editor, Frank Curran, was either on holidays or out sick, I got thrust into the maelstrom of the Troubles for real in the first week of February 1982 when I was appointed Editor. Suddenly, the realisation hit that the days of deflecting accountability, of blaming others for mistakes are over. You are it, you are The Editor, it's your responsibility.

And I have no hesitation whatsoever in stating to this day, I still struggle to describe the reality of those days. Where do you find the language to adequately describe how the totally abnormal had become the normal? Shootings, bombings, kneecappings, whole areas of the city no-go areas. This wasn't the norm in Dublin, Derby or Kerry - but it was in Derry.

The greats of literature would, believe me, struggle to get across on paper the visceral nature of life, the 'feel' as it were, of the place at that time. Try defining what is indefinable? The only real explanation is that you had to be there.

It was a surreal experience seeing heavily-armed soldiers running on the streets, police travelling in land rovers that clearly weighed almost as much as a tank, barricades at street corners, house raids in the middle of the night, hearing gunshots at rare hours

And yet, in the midst of all that, people had to get on with their everyday lives. As the wonderful Derry Girls so brilliantly portrayed, we worried about our children if they were late home from school. Were they caught in a bomb? Had they been 'lifted' by British soldiers? And in the midst of all this too…. What about their 11-Plus results?... Their 'A' Level results? ...Their job prospects?

The spark that many believe lit the whole conflagration that was to become the Troubles was the truly scandalous, sectarian decision to site Northern Ireland's second university not in the second city, Derry, but in the small unionist market town of Coleraine. It was an outrageous, politically-motivated decision made by a unionist regime at Stormont determined at all costs to keep Catholic/Nationalist Derry in the doldrums.

It is a scandal that continues in that, more than half a century later, it remains a wrong that has still to be righted.

Despite numerous promises made over the years by both politicians and academic bodies, the development of the city's Magee University campus borders on comedic. There is no development; in fact, there is a chance of regression.

And that old sore, emigration, is still rampant for young people looking for a job to match their qualifications and their skill set.

Perhaps saddest of all is that the three main institutions of society here have all massively declined in power and influence.

As leader of the biggest nationalist party at that time, the SDLP, Hume bestrode the political corridors of power in Britain, Europe and the US like a colossus. He, almost single-handedly, got the EU to invest in 'peace projects' in both the North and cross-border. He got American presidents directly involved in the peace process, culminating in Bill Clinton's acknowledged key role in getting the IRA ceasefire over the line.

Derry's centre-stage political status is no more. No political figure locally these days comes even close in terms of Hume's clout and influence. The same holds true of the Catholic Church. Bishop Daly had massive influence in the city of Derry and further afield not only because of his role as a prince of the church but because of his heroic actions on Bloody Sunday. He also knew how to use the power of the church to communicate. He was both a spiritual leader and a political leader in that he frequently condemned violence and was often in conflict with the leaders of the Republican Movement. He used the Journal so much that local wags often used to refer to the paper as the 'Daly Journal'. Scandals across the world have, of course, also played a part in the decline of the Catholic Church's power and influence.

And, of course, the Journal itself, once 'the bible' in Derry– as I heard it described on numerous occasions – has been badly hit by the many changes in our industry.

With little access to the levers of power in a tightly controlled political and media environment in Northern Ireland, particularly in the 1950s and 60s, the Derry Journal gave a public voice to the voiceless, giving the Catholic/Nationalist community a much-needed outlet to air their grievances with regard to the clear and undisputed bigotry and sectarian discrimination of the unionist state. Because of this, the paper was regularly attacked by those same institutions and was, on several occasions, banned by various NI Home Secretaries. That alone bears ample testimony to its recognised power and influence.

Today too, thanks to the perfect storm of increasing broadcast and social media, political changes etc, its influence and circulation have, like so many other newspapers, been adversly affected.

My life as Editor was lived in very different times - a time when Derry, which really should have been little more than a backwater city in the remote North-West corner of Ireland, was often centre stage across the globe.

HE WALKED ON WATER

I was sitting at home enjoying a quiet Saturday afternoon relaxing when Rosie called out that Hume was on the phone. I wasn't exactly dancing with delight. Free time was rare and all the more precious because of that. Never one for a lot of small talk, John got straight to the point: 'Are you about tomorrow night? I am hosting a dinner in Restaurant St John. Bring the wife.'

It turned out Hume had invited us to a private dinner for Kerry Kennedy, daughter of Robert F. Kennedy and niece of President John F. Kennedy. Back then in Irish society the Kennedys were on a par with the Holy Trinity. There was fawning coverage of them in the media, colour articles taking up full pages in the various Sunday papers indicating they were the nearest thing we had to Irish royalty. That they were also major players in the political life of the most powerful nation on the planet was also not to be sneezed at.

Amongst the 'A' list guests at an exclusive little restaurant that night were a Finnish cabinet minister, at least one ambassador – possibly two, and the playwright Brian Friel whose play 'Translations' had opened to world acclaim on Broadway some time earlier.

This was normal Hume territory, a man up among the gods. His status, already high, rose, almost perceptibly – nearly on a daily basis – so much so that he subsequently was to become Irish Man of the Century, win the Nobel Peace Prize, and be awarded honorary doctorates from just about every prestigious university in the world.

Let's not forget either this was a man on first name terms with presidents, prime ministers and media moguls. In every sense he really was a friend of the rich and powerful.

And if that wasn't enough, to top it all he was the local MP as well as being leader of the North's biggest nationalist party, the SDLP.

Yet, for some reason that I have never got to the bottom of, we never quite clicked. I didn't really get on all that well with him. I don't know if it was a clash of personalities or whether I didn't see the world from his perspective, but we were to be tuned to different frequencies on many issues, both political and social.

In terms of being Editor of the Journal, the smart move on my part would have been to ensure I was in his inner circle, to keep on his right side – but in truth I never made much of an effort. To this day I can't give a rational answer but somewhere in the back of my head I believed the Alex Ferguson dictum during the Manchester United glory days was the correct one; Fergie held that a bit of distance from the players was vital for perspective.

I needed that distance from Hume, as I was of the opinion the paper had almost crossed over from reporting to hagiography when it came to coverage of him.

As far as I could ascertain, Hume was God in Derry. It seemed to me that many people were accepting his judgements and opinions without question. I had first-hand experience of this when on one memorable occasion in my presence he totally slapped down a senior SDLP person who didn't even so much as raise a word by way of objection after making what I regarded as a totally legitimate point. I thought, what a doormat to accept being slapped down publicly like that.

I never had that kind of personality to accept this kind of approach. I believed we had the right – a duty even, high-minded as that might sound – to report impartially when other voices criticised him. Or when others offered a different analysis or viewpoint. Because of that we clashed on occasions.

I am not suggesting for a second this was all Hume's fault. Far from it. My own views, attitude and personality probably had a lot to do with our clashes.

From the outset I was aware Hume had a very tight-knit circle, and power in Derry belonged within that circle. His grouping consisted in the main of members of the professional classes - doctors, lawyers and accountants - many of whom, or so it seemed to me, reflected the views of only a certain section of the community.

They all grew up together, went to the same school, knew each other, drank together, partied together, and their families frequently intermingled at weddings, funerals and the various religious and social occasions.

I used to, privately, call them 'the St. Columb's College Ruling Class', as that was the alma mater of those who passed the 11-Plus and became the elite of Derry.

A respected colleague of mine explained years later that this was a trait in some St Columb's guys of that generation, massively arrogant because of their first-class education, and yet massively insecure because of their religion and second-class status in a unionist-dominated society.

I soon became aware that while old money and a posh accent might have been the definer of social class in other areas under the British state, in Derry being a past pupil of St Columb's seemed to be a prerequisite for this particular 'old boys' club. Once you were in, doors opened. Though in saying that this wasn't true for everyone who attended St. Columb's - not in the least - but rather for the select few.

As Derry was pretty parochial back then, being a Donegal man probably didn't help. The Columb's cohort had learned to play the game in the North and knew the rules. I hardly knew the game, much less the rules. And the times, as Bob Dylan had written not that many years earlier, really were 'a changing'.

The vice-like grip of the old unionist party was starting to be pulled off the neck of the Catholic community. This group of young, ambitious, well-educated Derry men were the vanguard of nationalism, the first grouping to scent political power and were hungry for it. And Hume was out front, their leader.

For me, it was all new and so, so very different from life in the South.

It took time to get my head around how different society twenty miles up the road from where I was reared really was.

Partition had created many differences, not least the evolution of two very different ways of educating children. In the South free education had opened doors to everyone, irrespective of financial restrictions or academic ability. Success was available in Donegal to all academically – I, personally, was walking, living proof of this – whereas in the North the 11-Plus 'selected' the few at the top and channelled the rest to be, in the main, the worker bees of society.

It struck me quite forcibly that this streaming system was perfectly acceptable to the Catholics who passed the 11-Plus. Indeed, as far as I was concerned, they were way too comfortable with this. And that included the Catholic clergy.

They had bought into it as it worked for them.

They never seemed to see - wilfully so, I believed then and to this day - that this was another form of discrimination in that it continually advantaged the better off . Stupid children of the rich could get grinds and pass the exam; bright children of the less well-off were rarely, if ever, able to avail of such expensive assistance.

This was confirmed to me by many teachers I got to know who contended not only was the exam deeply flawed - it was a kind of rote exam which did not determine a broader intelligence – but was also unfair to the less well-off. The Johnny Dohertys and the Mickey McDaids in the Bog or the Creggan rarely, if ever, got the same kind of breaks to help them over the finish line.

Very much part of that elite circle of Catholic families were the McCarrolls who owned the Journal. While nominally described as nationalist, as F.E.

McCarroll had been a Nationalist Party councillor for a time, they were, in my view, conservative golf club types. The old definition of the Alliance Party - middle class, middle aged and middle of the road – was, I would contend, a perfect summation for their outlook. Radicals like Martin McGuinness or Eamonn McCann were, from their viewpoint, little more than troublemakers at best or subversives at worst, though the McCarrolls did become much more receptive to both as the years passed.

Non-threatening Hume was their man as, indeed, he was the man of the middle classes in their private homes on the Culmore Road.

In the working-class estates like Creggan and Bogside, which bore the brunt of much of the British security authorities oppression, the view was far from uniform. I learned this within weeks of taking over. It was clear the ground was beginning to shift away from the previously all-dominant SDLP, that they didn't speak for everyone. It was abundantly clear too many of the folks who lived in the huge estates felt left behind and alienated. The fact I could catch on to this so quickly caused me some surprise when I found the SDLP people I spoke to seemed oblivious to it.

In conversations both within and without the Derry Journal I learned this feeling of not being listened to, of being taken for granted in terms of voting was deeply resented. I heard it repeatedly in the early days that the Journal reflected the views of those in the 'the Catholic Club' not the housing estates.

I had no problem accepting that this was an accurate reflection of the political reality as I believed it myself based on little more than the empirical evidence of having regular conversations and hearing how people felt truly pissed off.

That, however, was the macro issue I knew would have to be dealt with in the longer term.

The micro issue – and by far the main one for me personally – began within weeks of taking over as Editor. I had to address this one head on.

Hume, basically, made the same speech everywhere he went. He topped and tailed it to suit the occasion, but the core of the text was always the same. I can still remember its cliché-ridden sentences ....'the land of Ireland is united, it's the people who are divided', 'let's spill our sweat not our blood', 'difference is the essence of humanity, difference is an accident of birth...and should therefore never be a source of hatred or conflict.' And on it went along those lines.

Academically rigorous it most certainly was; profound too, but I had heard it so often I could have recited it verbatim as a party piece.

But irrespective of the fact that it was that same stump speech every time, he expected it to be the lead story in the Derry Journal every week. It might have been the UN or Washington or the University of Notre Dame, but it was always the same speech.

And I knew from talking to staff that they just skipped it, that for most it was a total non-story in news terms. If they were ignoring it, I could only presume readers were doing the same.

After a lot of thought on how best to approach this problem, long before my first year as Editor was out I had told Hume, during a somewhat heated discussion, I wasn't putting the same statement in each time simply because his name was on it, even if he was delivering it for the first time at the White House, the European Parliament or whereever.

Despite my best efforts to explain that I had totally legitimate journalistic reasons for my decision – virtually the same story in time after time was a total non-runner – he was having none of it. He was the local MP. He was the leader of nationalism. He demanded that he be given prominence. He left very angry.

I knew I was breaking the mould here, and that what I was doing was risky. The Editor before me, Frank Curran, a Derry city native much more attuned to the local power player, had had a different, much more mellow approach.

He was an absolutely superb journalist and a seriously bright man. Indeed, he was the only man I knew who could do his own tax returns and get money back from the Revenue Authorities. With an ability like that he should have been a high-flying accountant.

In his early twenties he had written a superb book, *Ireland's Fascist City*, which exposed the malign influence of the local unionist group, the Faceless Men, whose raison d'etre was to ensure Derry remained unionist, got no investment so that the local nationalist population would be kept poor and see emigration as their only outlet.

He was later to write the definitive account of what led to the outbreak of the Troubles in *Derry, Countdown to Disaster,* which has become almost a seminal text for those trying to understand what brought the war in the North into being.

But by the time he became Editor – he was in his mid-50s – he was no longer interested in radicalisation and had, whether by accident or design, adopted a laissez-faire editorial policy when it came to local figures of influence. He just kept doing what the editors before him had been doing.

I understood where he was coming from. It made for an easier life. And while it was easy for 'young me' to judge, it is not insignificant that I myself had retired from the Editor's Chair by the time I was 52.

In Frank's time, if Hume wasn't on the front page there would be a fair chance Bishop Daly would be. And if not Daly, some SDLP councillor would get pride of place. That was how the game at that time was being played.

But considering what was happening in the city and across the North - the hunger strikes were changing the dynamics of politics across the entire island - I didn't regard that as a road I could realistically go down.

It might have been naïve to toss the applecart so radically but the fire of youth was still burning bright in my journalistic soul. Putting in a stale statement just because of who had issued it was, as far as I was concerned, partisan party PR masquerading as journalism, and I decided it was a game I was not prepared to play.

I held the view that the reader was not an idiot, that there was an awareness that everything was either changed or changing. They would know when we published almost unchallenged old traditional views that we had opted for the line of least resistance rather than rattle the cages that needed rattled.

It was clear too in my mind the 'who' was no longer as important, on many occasions, when it came to deciding what made a good lead story; the 'what' or the 'why' was often far more revealing.

What was a previously almost politically-dormant Sinn Fein up to now? Why were they changing rapidly? They had gone for a grassroots approach and new advice centres were springing up in the big housing estates right across the city. What was that all about? Why was the DUP opposing a GAA pitch in the Waterside? Why did Gerry O'Grady, of the Alliance Party, live in a staunchly republican area where every time he put a statement in the Journal it was not uncommon to risk a stone through his window? His grit and courage were to be admired.

Those were the sort of stories I wanted to get people talking about.

Readers had read far too many versions, I believed, of 'let's spill our sweat not our blood' not that that wasn't important, just that it wasn't news anymore.

One other significant editorial decision I took was if Sinn Fein or the IRA issued a major statement of interest, I would run it as lead. If young DUP firebrand Gregory Campbell had something to say he would be on the front page too.

To my knowledge few, if any, unionists had the lead story in the Journal before I arrived.

Needless to say, Hume didn't like this new editorial policy, accusing me more than once of not understanding local dynamics or, as things got more heated as the weeks went by, of being some kind of republican sympathiser, and it wasn't too long before he was ringing up – or some of his supporters were - claiming the 'Journal' was undermining him, that Sinn Fein was getting more coverage than he was.

I let it go for quite a time hoping the tumult would subside, but it got so patently ridiculous when I had a lengthy heated exchange with him that I decided to go through back issues of the papers around this time. Following this little bit of research, I sent him a reply pointing out that, of about the previous twenty-five/twenty-six editions he had been on the front page on about eighteen of them - if not the lead story every time, at least on the early pages. It made little difference to his attitude. As far as John was concerned, he felt he should have been front page on all twenty-six.

I was only too aware I was on shaky ground. For a young editor in his early days this was not the start I needed. Far from it, and I knew it was a matter of time before it would come to a head. And at least I was proved 100% right on that if nothing else.

Despite having a Friday off I always called in to the office to pick up a copy of the paper and to check for any urgent messages. This particular Friday morning I called in only to be met by Colm McCarroll, and it was clear he had been waiting on me. While he had been one of my most ardent supporters in pushing me for the Editor's job, from his demeanour it was patently obvious he was not a happy camper.

Without any preamble he said he and his father wanted a 'clear the air' meeting with me as they had a number of concerns about that particular morning's edition.

I knew this was it - make or break day had arrived.

At that meeting Colm, the then heir apparent to succeed his father as boss, started by informing me that the view 'out on the golf course' the previous night was that the Journal was turning into little more than the Derry version of Sinn Fein's in-house publication, 'An Phoblacht'. And that morning's paper confirmed, he asserted, they were right.

This, to me, was like a red rag to a bull, so I asked could he tell me the names of his golf course buddies who had been whispering in his ear? He did so, and on learning one particular name I suggested that our conversation was bordering on the ridiculous. I countered that he was suggesting my editorship policy should be determined by the views of a group of Pringle-wearing Alliance types at City of Derry Golf Club?

And, on a bit of an angry roll by now, I pointed out a golf course was hardly a true representative sampling area for the views of the people of Derry. I also pointed out, none too subtly, that both he and they were out of touch with what was happening on the ground. Could he explain how in some estates Sinn Fein was now getting up to 30% of the vote?

That fact seemed to take both McCarrolls by surprise.

While, most definitely, decent people on many, many levels the McCarrolls lived parallel lives to most people in the sprawling estates. They lived in good homes in the exclusive areas of the city untouched by security force raids, drove expensive cars, stayed in nice hotels whilst off on various golfing weekends, were scratch golfers and, in addition, could afford to holiday regularly on the Continent. By way of contrast, in some of the huge, sprawling estates up to 80% of the male population was unemployed and a day out to Buncrana was a big deal.

I could tell there was a definite turning of the tide in the room, so I threw in a couple of observations along the lines that a youngster born at the outbreak of the Troubles no longer had the same respect for the old ruling establishment as their parents, that the old deference to traditional authority figures was gone.

As Editor, I explained, these were the issues worthy of reporting and exploration.

Finally, I put my last throw of the dice out on the table.

I explained that, for me, there was a very simple principle in regard to news – one they could judge for themselves. And it was this – the best story, irrespective of its source, would be the lead in each and every edition under my editorship.

The dynamic I wanted, I explained, was for the paper to have an edge, to lead public opinion not simply reflect it. I thought that was the only way forward for the paper, and for me as Editor.

And I went for broke in a high stakes move – if they didn't agree, I would move on. I made it clear what I was saying wasn't meant as a threat – I most certainly didn't want to lose my job – but what I was saying I believed to be both authentic and accurate. And I wasn't going to be side-tracked by a few golfers.

It was to prove a watershed moment.

Frank McCarroll senior, the then boss, ended the discussion almost immediately. He had no problem with what I had said in regard to the Journal's new editorial policy. Indeed, he said, he totally agreed with it. He made it clear as long as he, as the newspaper proprietor, could point to all and sundry that our headline story was the best, most important story in that edition he would support that.

And he then did something much more important, when he pointedly asked: 'Isn't that right, Colm?' sending his son – in my opinion – a signal to say there would be no further discussion. No more interference with the Editor.

I was to come to admire this man tremendously. In the years that followed he never deviated from this stance. He was a man of his word. And he supported me in so many other ways as well that I only ever think of him to this day with kindness and gratitude. Colm, to be fair to him, would come to respect and defend my stance, and from that day forward, I never heard another word from the golf club press corps.

As for Hume, in later years we sorted ourselves out and worked reasonably well together. He mentioned this phase of our relationship on several occasions, and he went out of his way on those occasions to tell me he hadn't complained to the proprietor or his family, but I have little doubt that he did. If he was complaining so vociferously not only to me but also to many others, it's inconceivable he wasn't complaining to them.

In retrospect Hume and I worked with each other on a professional level, but we were never going to be best friends or drinking buddies though, to contradict myself, I did go for a drink with him on several occasions.

Hume's public image, the 'Saint John' so beloved by the Irish Times, RTE and others was not always matched in private. In his autobiography, John Major, described the SDLP leader as 'prickly' and I have no reason to dispute that description. He could often be tetchy and, on occasions, arrogant. Locally, as I have already stated, he expected unquestioning support, and took a dim view of those who might dare to stray from the prevailing orthodoxy as decided by him.

A prime example of these characteristics was to the forefront one day when Hume, myself and Martin Cowley, who had been London Editor of the 'Irish Times' back in the 1970s, went for lunch in the Everglades Hotel in Derry. It's worth pointing out we went to the Everglades because it was the only hotel in the city, the IRA having bombed the others to smithereens.

We had a nice time. Hume, often morose and taciturn, actually in quite an upbeat mood but as we were leaving, he called Martin aside and they were gone for about five minutes.

'What was that about?' I asked Cowley when he returned noting his far from happy expression as he re-joined me in the car park outside the hotel. Martin, the mildest and most decent of people, looked more than a little annoyed..

He explained he had written a major profile article for the Op-Ed section of the 'Irish Times' on Hume the previous weekend, which was very well received. He tried to give a little bit of colour to the private man rather than just the famous politician. In it he had thrown in a line that the renowned, serious - minded politico liked a drink and a song when relaxing with family and friends. He thought this little bit of incidental detail would humanise him, make him more sympathetic.

But Hume didn't see it like that. He was a politician with serious status and didn't want anything to detract from that image.

I can only presume Martin had originally thought he was getting called aside to be thanked and was not expecting the slap down in regard to a few minor asides.

It was something I too had come across - no thanks for the substantive coverage, picky criticism for the things he didn't like. That could be Hume.

It should be pointed out that years later the more mellow Hume proved Martin right as he was regularly seen in various hostelries in Derry and Donegal singing and enjoying a jar.

'The Town I Loved So Well' was his favourite party piece, regularly performed for visiting Americans.

The years passed and Hume invited me to come to Europe with him, so in 1995 I went to Strasbourg. It was around June, so I took my wife, Rosie, and two youngest kids with me and made it our summer holiday for that year.

While there he was a really attentive host, making a real effort to ensure we had a good time. In great humour on one occasion, he gave the security guards at the parliament the slip when he rushed on to the floor of the chamber holding my youngest son's hand. As only elected members were supposed to be on this hallowed ground they were quickly ushered out, but son Paddy still has that claim to fame.

And by his reaction it was only too clear Hume thoroughly enjoyed that bit of fun too. He had that side to him.

We also met all sorts of characters and top personalities during this visit and generally enjoyed the experience. When I came back, I wrote up the article and, not unexpectedly, gave Hume the starring role. He rang up the following week about another issue but just before putting down the phone remarked, 'Oh, by the way – loved the article on our visit to Strasbourg.'

I'm pretty certain in my 25 years as Editor of the Derry Journal it was the only time I ever got thanked, that is if 'loved the article' counts as thanks.

He's gone now, and the world is definitely a much poorer place for his passing.

I have no hesitation in saying he was an absolute political colossus. For his intellectual genius and heroic courage, he deserves every plaudit under the sun.

He was a true one-off, the central figure who devised the strategy that eventually gave peace to Northern Ireland.

The stress he was under on a daily basis had to be seen at first hand to be fully understood. I think this affected him very deeply, and affected his relationships with a number of people, me included. I have to own up to the fact that it took me years to be compassionate enough to understand that. All I saw for quite a while was an often-narky man giving me a hard time. Looking in the rear-view mirror I realise I was often short-sighted and should have been more generous. I regret that now.

I would, however, be a liar if I tried to paint a picture of him as an easy man to deal with. I never found that.

But it's worth putting on the record that we finished on good terms.

On my final day as Editor of the Derry Journal, Hume landed down in the office trying to hide a present clearly visible under his coat. Out it came, a bottle of very rare whiskey from a specially distilled cask given to him in honour of his having won the Nobel Peace Prize. This was a very, very limited-edition whiskey and much sought after. It was very, very decent of him. He often hid that decency, that kind of generosity, under that prickly personality.

THE BOY GENERAL

Shortly after I was appointed Editor a former priest, Paddy Logue, came to see me and said Martin McGuinness would like to meet me, and was it okay if he brought him down the next day? I replied I would look forward to it.

Back then if this was a Hollywood western, the director would have had Hume wearing a white hat – the good guy – and the baddie, who always wore a black hat, would have been McGuinness. So, I was intrigued to meet him.

Though still only in his early thirties Martin McGuinness was already a living legend, mentioned in newspaper articles and books across the globe. For many he was a living Che Guevara. With his curly blond hair and piercing eyes, he had the film star looks that intrigued the media.

The background story of McGuinness is well documented. He left school early, ending up working in the local firm of James Doherty and Sons, Butchers. He didn't get his 11-Plus, didn't go to the elite local St Columb's College, alma mater to Hume, Heaney, Friel et al, didn't go to university and his world view of what was happening around him was very different to Hume's.

While Hume was world famous for his peace efforts McGuinness was world famous for his war efforts. I openly admit to being more than a little daunted at the prospect of meeting him for the first time.

My big problem was he wasn't in the least like I had expected. Not even close.

The IRA terrorism chief, Martin McGuinness I met that next day and was to get to know well over the years totally threw a spanner in my world of stereotypes. McGuinness didn't drink or smoke, didn't mess around with women, had a lovely family and, I was to learn from empirical experience, kept his word. Well, to me he did. He came from what would be known locally as 'respectable people', his parents noted for their decency and their adherence to their Catholic faith. Both were not only daily mass goers but, I was told often, were also daily communicants.

McGuinness came to politics through the streets, through activism – not ideology. He told me this many times. And in an article written in 1988 – in his own handwriting and before the advent of the ubiquitous press release - for the Derry Journal, on the 20th Anniversary of the Civil Rights March of 1968, he explained it was the treatment meted out to nationalist leaders, people like veteran National Party leader Eddie McAteer, by members of the RUC that made him realise that they held all nationalists/Catholics in contempt.

He said that had changed him totally, that it was his road to Damascus moment, a seminal event in the life of a young man who grew up apolitical, 'without a care in the world' as he put it then, in Derry's Bogside in the early 1960s. I remember almost verbatim what he said about it: 'If they could do that to our leaders – people I looked up to, really no one in our community is safe or respected.'

Some months later the British army killed two young Derry men in highly controversial circumstances and McGuinness told me that was it - he made up his mind he was joining the IRA.

Despite his lack of formal educational qualifications McGuinness was highly intelligent. Indeed, all around he was way more complex than the box I had mentally tried to put him in. I had massive moral issues with him, and it took me a long time to adjust. How could I have come to not only like but genuinely respect a man who was regarded as a murderer by so many? How could such an obviously honourable man on a personal level lead an organisation that planted bombs under cars that blew people to bits?

To me it was a massive paradox, and it had my head in a spin.

The only explanation I can give is that we, literally, spent hundreds of hours talking over the years and the guarded conversations of our early days soon opened up to full on discussions where nothing was held back. I like to believe I got to know the real Martin McGuinness. What drove him was moral certitude. He believed totally in the righteousness of his cause, that we were engaged in a war with the forces of oppression and subjugation and that fighting that war was a just cause. He made no apologies. The forces of the British State were so massive, so superior, that the only way to fight them was, he told me, by using tactics that they liked to call 'terrorism'.

'How long do you think we would last if we fought a pitch battle with them?' I recall him asking me one day, before he added: 'We have to fight them on our terms, not theirs.' And fight they most certainly did.

I suppose the best way I can describe him is that he was the Michael Collins of our generation. And that's how I came to see him.

It was a long journey for me to 'get' the real Martin McGuinness. As a good Catholic boy brought up in a home where in childhood, we said the Rosary every evening, I had trouble for years finding the round hole in my brain in which I could fit this so-called 'terrorist' in a square box. I was far from alone in my dilemma. I saw and heard evidence of this over the years as Martin emerged from the shadows into political life.

But that was still a long way down the line.

When Hume came down to the office the proprietors would go out of their way to speak with him, when McGuinness arrived, they made sure to make themselves scarce. And on the staff, there were some who clearly hero-worshipped McGuinness while others made clear their detestation. He was definitely a polarising figure.

I can only state that in all my dealings with him over twenty-five years he was never less than honourable. In my dealings with him he was neither a thug nor a bully. Many were the heated arguments and debates I had with him and not once did he raise his voice or lose his temper. That's a fact, something I, personally, can stand over.

Other people, obviously, have very different opinions.

Seeing that I could hardly explain or comprehend my own opinion of the 'Boy General' – as one of the reporters used to always describe him – needless to say I found it almost impossible to explain to people, even to close family, that the media image and the reality of the man were so far removed as to be bordering on the risible.

I eventually all but stopped trying as my attempts were often met with derision by people within my circle who formed the view that I had been brainwashed by dangerous subversives. Without ever meeting the man they preferred to believe the caricatures of McGuinness in the Sunday Independent or the other Dublin papers, articles often written by people who pontificated about him but had never, ever met him.

One particularly glaring example of this kind of journalism, which stands out for me, was when the Sunday Times' Northern Editor, the late Liam Clarke, one of the most trenchant critics of McGuinness, came to the Bogside for a public meeting.

I happened to be on the panel that evening, and prior to the meeting I was standing beside Liam. When McGuinness came in he shook hands with various people including Liam and it was only too clear they had never met or, as far as I could tell, talked one-on-one. Yet Clarke was the guy writing so-called expert analysis pieces almost week in, week out on what he was up to and what tactics and strategy he was devising for the Republican movement.

And to this day all I will say is who am I to disabuse those people of their prejudices?

During our often-protracted conversations I tried on more than one occasion to get him to explain why he joined the IRA, why he hadn't gone down the

Hume route. Again, I have no difficulty in recalling his response as it has stayed in my mind over the years.

I remember conversations like this almost verbatim: 'In every society in a time of oppression there will be those who cooperate with the oppressors for their own benefit; there'll be others who put their heads down and try and get through it; there'll be some who quietly oppose it in subtle ways; and then there will the others, usually the minority, who'll openly fight physical force oppression with physical force. We all make our choices.'

History will record very clearly what option Martin McGuinness took.

If a shorthand explanation is of any benefit the best way to explain the political bifurcation in Derry at the time was like this - if John Hume was Derry's 'ying' Martin McGuinness was its 'yang'. They were, in many ways, the personification of the dichotomy that was the political struggle for many people. They were colossal figures in the same city but lived very different lives.

One final thing - the late Dr. Tom McGinley, a well-respected GP in one of the biggest medical practices in Derry, perhaps summed it up best when one day we had a discussion in my office. McGinley, no supporter of physical violence, told me he always had had a major dilemma equating the quiet, well-mannered young man who sat waiting his turn at the Aberfoyle Surgery with the terror chief as portrayed in the British media. McGuinness, he said, was 'polite, well mannered, waited his turn, and spoke respectfully to everyone'.

That was the Martin McGuinness I knew.

A TWIST OF FATE

I was in the press gallery in Dail Eireann when one of the uniformed attendants came on to the gallery to inform me that there was 'a fella from the Derry Journal' on the phone in the press room who had asked for me by name.

When I got to the phone Colm McCarroll's first words were 'You are a hard man to get….' To put this comment in context, this was the era before mobile phones and in those days you could wait, literally so, for years in certain parts of the country for the installation of a landline. We had real experience of how bad the communications systems were in the country when for several months after moving to Dublin, when we wanted to contact people at home, we had to go to a public phone box near where we lived in Ballinteer.

The fact that Colm had phoned RTE headquarters several times, had been given the runaround on every occasion before, finally, being told to try Dáil Éireann suggested to me that he really was keen to talk about me joining the Journal. After a short conversation he ended the call with, 'Next time you are up home give me a shout and we'll have a good talk about you coming on board.'

I knew instinctively this would be the defining decision of my working life. It was 'Die dog, or shite the license' time.

I had started off life heading, possibly, into accountancy but fallen into journalism almost by default. But once in the door I knew I had found my niche. Hard to believe but at one stage accountancy looked like being my fate but I can state with certainty I would have been a disaster in that profession. I didn't have the mental make-up for it. My brain was not geared to the onerous, unending monotony of double-entry bookkeeping or cost accountancy where the only words I recall now despite months of studying the subject are Lifo (Last in first Out) and Fifo (First in, first out). To paraphrase Yeats, 'adding the halfpence to the pence' was never going to be my role in life. Of that I was certain.

However, failing Maths in my Leaving Certificate meant my educational options were somewhat limited back in 1971. It was pretty certain Oxford and Cambridge were not coming a-knocking so for me it was a case of accepting whatever was being offered, not what I wanted or would like.

Growing up in the early 1960s it would not be inaccurate to describe Letterkenny as a backwater, an economically-depressed blackspot with no real industry. Job opportunities were few. Like so many of my counterparts who hadn't hit the academic high spots, I had vague plans about possibly emigrating. My mother, however, a firm believer in education, was having none of it.

'There's that new college opening out the road - you can go there', she said one day out of the blue, not even knowing what that new college was called. Neither did I. That college is now the pristine Atlantic Technological University but was then known as the Donagh O'Malley Regional Technical College or, to us, colloquially 'the RTC'. All I will say now is how I gained entrance to that college couldn't be done today.

With the realisation in that late summer of 1971 that prevarication had to end, I walked out to the college to see what they had to offer. It was a belting hot day so I'm thinking it was probably late August.

I saw this man wiping the glass up around the front door. Presuming he was the caretaker I casually strolled over and asked, 'Who do you have to talk-to to get in here?' 'Me' came the response.

It was none other than the president of the college, Dr. Dan O'Hare. He was a one-man band - president, registrar, receptionist and, in those days, seemingly caretaker and groundsman.

It was all too obvious the college wasn't physically ready, but they were going ahead with the opening anyway. Not only were there some rooms unpainted, some had a limited supply of chairs and when classes got underway just a couple of weeks later, it was clear, as I later learned, they also had real problems in regard to staffing.

One lecturer, Peadar Mulligan, a Ballybofey man, as I recall, taught just about every subject for quite a while. He did the accountancy, the economics, even the maths though he often needed the help of Columba Bonnar who had somehow fallen through the academic floor despite being highly intelligent. This really was education at the primitive, pioneering end.

But, again, I'm getting ahead of myself.

On that first day, in we went to Dr. O'Hare's inner sanctum that passed for his office and I noted the breeze-block outer wall was so bad it looked like it came straight from a cheap Australian TV soap. A small kitchen-type table passed for his desk. And as he was seated, I had the choice of one other (plastic) chair - or the floor. I felt for a couple of minutes that I should be interviewing him to determine whether the RTC was up to my standards but then in a moment of glittering reality I remembered my standards were exactly matched by this building – basic.

He asked for my Leaving Cert results, and while no expert on body language I could see he was noticeably under-whelmed. I would presume he quickly figured with my Maths results, engineering or physics were not really options. But after noting I had got good results in Economics, English and History it was decided I would be a suitable candidate for the Business Studies department.

And that was that.

I was now entering another significant stage of life. And what I didn't realise at that time was so was Letterkenny. Like the rest of the country, it was beginning to benefit from the policies of former Taoiseach Sean Lemass who had ditched Eamon de Valera's vision of rural Ireland where comely maidens danced at the crossroads for a more pragmatic version where jobs and economic growth took priority. Now this little rural backwater was on the cusp of massive change. Few of us, none maybe, at that time saw it coming, much less understood how rapid change was going to be.

The town I grew up in was an almost 100 per cent homogeneous society where strangers stood out. I am open to correction, but I think there was only one black person living in the town then; as far I'm aware he had met and married a Letterkenny woman in England who had insisted they return to her home place.

But now there was talk of a big factory and a new college, and people in our small, rural town were totally blind to what a third level college and a state-of-the-art Courtaulds factory, opening almost simultaneously, would bring.

Almost 100 percent Catholic and conservative it was shell-shocked by the hundreds of young people who moved in almost overnight – the drinking, the partying, the lifestyles, were like a thunderbolt.

The college, in particular, was a real catalyst for change. One of the claims that went viral – and this was long before social media – was that the female partner of one of the new lecturers, he was a hippy sort of guy – used to walk around the house nude on occasions. This could have been fair enough except there were no curtains on the windows. Some others alleged another lecturer had a bronze cast of her backside in the front hallway of her home. In view of the fact that most homes in the area would have had a statue of the Sacred Heart in a prominent place these were truly shocking departures from the norm.

I suppose the 'Swinging Sixties' had finally arrived in Donegal, albeit almost a decade late.

And it brought with a cohort of people that shook the place up. The head of Business Studies, Ray Patten, was a particularly good example of what this group of weird and wonderful characters did to startle the fuddy-duddy attitudes of what had once been a sleepy country town.

Despite having zero background or support locally Ray ran as a candidate for Independent Fianna Fail in the Letterkenny Urban Council elections in the mid-1970s and got all of 36 votes. How a man with a plummy English accent, all the characteristics of an old fogey British colonel, ended up running for an avowedly republican party during a time of major strife in the North is still a mystery. But the craic was great.

Amongst his many idiosyncrasies – his car was something out of the 1940s - he frequently abbreviated words, often with hilarious results. One day he walked into the lecture hall and announced to us: 'You lot are having French with sex.'

The unanimous response was a quizzical 'what?'

It was, I presume, a real disappointment when they learned they were having French with the sec(retarial) class.

And, for a young lad like myself in a new institution, I soon learned it attracted a diverse range of students.

One day I was walking out to college and for some strange reason I got talking to another student about poitín.

'I have never tasted poitín,' I said.

With that he stopped, opened up a rucksack and said: 'Take a sip of that.'

Where he got it from, why he was bringing it into college and how I ended up tasting poitín at 9:15 on a wet autumn morning in 1971, I'll never be able to explain.

And there was Roger Regan, a classmate, who was the first ever president of the students' union. He was a true one-off. The son of a well-known local solicitor, the story goes after he left the college he was sitting in a pub in London, overheard a man say he needed a gang of plasterers for a big job coming up, and Roger jumped over a couple of seats to tell him he could do it.

Despite never having plastered a day in his life Roger, apparently, rounded up a navvy gang of hard-drinking, hardworking Irish men by scouring the pubs in the area over the weekend and got the start on a Monday morning. By all accounts he did the job - and many others – afterwards and made himself a small fortune along the way.

I heard some years back – we are talking 30 years at this stage - he was living in Geelong, outside of Melbourne, but I have since learned that he has passed.

I suppose many things coalesce to shape a life even if you are unaware of it at the time. During these student days I used to earn a bit of pocket money by working as a barman at the Continental Bar in the town's Lr Main St. It was owned by John Devine who was a bit of a character. He really put into practice that much overused cliché of thinking outside the box. Some years before I started working there, he had opened up one of the first lounge bars in Donegal but when he ran out of money and couldn't furnish it, he extracted seats from an old Lough Swilly bus and set them on truncated wooden pallets around the tables. Comfortable yes, effective yes, class no.

It was, quite literally, shabby chic long before anyone had even coined the phrase.

At that time emigration was rife so we had any number of Americans calling in. One such visitor was a Cavan man, Pete O'Hanlon, who was married to a Letterkenny woman. Pete owned two bars in Queens, New York and like Devine was a bit of a character. I must have done something to impress him because one night John landed up at our house saying Pete was willing to offer me a summer job in America.

To this day my mother's reaction surprised me; she thought I should take it and go. This was a woman who was such a worrier she would have demanded you send a telegram or a letter to confirm where you were even if you were only going up to the next room, yet here she was willing to let me go to big bad New York.

I still can't fathom it.

It must have been heart-wrenching for her, but she sort of knew that the time to fly the nest was fast approaching. God love her! I know now how she must have felt then. Anyway, it all happened quickly that the big trip was on. And after much discussion it turned out that my brother, Hugh, would also be going along.

And so, on June 30th, 1972 off we headed to America. It was Hughie's 20th birthday that day, a day he – and myself! – have never forgotten. It was our first trip out of the country, and our first flight. And it turned out to be one hell of an experience.

The flight itself was the flight from hell.

Not too long out of Ireland we ran smack into the middle of what the pilot described as 'an electrical storm' – thunder and lightning. The turbulence was so severe it was like riding a bronco horse for the best part of an hour. On one occasion there were passengers screaming when the plane dropped like a stone some 600 metres after hitting some sort of air pocket.

Amongst the passengers were a large contingent of nuns and priests heading to the States to provide holiday cover for clergy in various Catholic parishes, and in my naivety about the dangers of flying I was wondering why they had all their rosary beads out and could be seen praying with considerable devotion. Little wonder when the plane landed there was one very long and sustained burst of applause, the relief clearly palpable. These days, caught in similar circumstances, I would be in need of oxygen and medical assistance. But my naivety was such that it was like water off a duck. I thought that flights like this were an everyday occurrence, not that the possibility of crashing had been very real.

On landing there was another, more mundane reality. No one had mentioned New York summers.

Our mother's insistence that we dress properly for the trip had unintended consequences. She didn't want us landing in America like some ne'er-do-well Irish poor that had left our shores generations before. So, she insisted we wear our top gear heavy tweed three-piece Donegal suits. They were not exactly designed for New York in late June.

Standing in the long security queue at Kennedy Airport I scanned a clock on the wall which said it was 102 degrees. But the real killer was the humidity. I was, quite literally, leaving little pools of water where I was standing.

As we stood in line to go through immigration, I noticed a black man dressed in T-shirt and shorts sweating profusely. He caught my eye, wiped his brow in a gesture to indicate heat and must have thought, 'Who let these clowns out dressed like that?'

It was to be a long summer. I spent three months there, living out on Long Island. It opened up my eyes to how backward, out of touch, for good or ill, Ireland was from what was happening in the big bad world. New York in 1972 was at the forefront of human experience – huge cars, high rise buildings, a melting pot of races, colours, vibrancy, fashion, culture and a whole attitude to life that was poles apart from rural Donegal. You could almost smell the wealth, the dynamism, the rat race of the ambitious to 'make it' there.

Culturally it was day and night. At home, Irish conservatism was still front and centre both politically and in the untrammelled power of the Catholic church. In New York it was said 'anything goes' and it sure did.

'Hair' the musical which featured full frontal nudity had opened on Broadway some years before. Back in Ireland women didn't even give a hint of cleavage yet that long hot summer the braless look was everywhere in New York. Remembering to keep your eyes on the face of a girl whose chest was clearly visible in an almost transparent t-shirt is, believe me, one of the most difficult tasks any 18-year-old Irish boy has ever had to do.

I was staying with my mother's best friend, Annie McMenamin, in a little town called Little Neck and before leaving to go visit New York she had warned me and Hughie to 'stay away from that dirty old Times Square – nothing but dirty old movie houses there.'

Guess where we went first? Yip, you are right – Times Square.

I had rarely seen a photograph of a naked woman much less a real live one, so our first movie was as much a biology lesson as a sexual experience. And there were sex shops with magazines for every taste. Believe me, there are some pretty weird people living in New York.

And on several street corners there were real pretty girls dolled up to the nines …it took me some time to realise they were 'working girls'. You didn't see that down the Main Street in Letterkenny.

Finding work that summer was good craic. It wasn't as easy as we were led to believe.

As my brother didn't have a work visa, he took the job working for Pete in his bar in Jamaica Avenue. It used to be an all-Irish part of the city but by then most of the Irish had moved up the social ladder and different communities had moved in. It could be dodgy on occasions.

I got a job working for a private security firm, Wackenhut, out on Bay Point. I had to wear the Wackenhut shirt, jacket and belt and as I travelled by public transport, I never realised that my uniform could be misinterpreted.

One night standing at the bus stop for a bus running late, a guy offered me a lift saying he was heading towards Little Neck. I thought what the hell, it beats waiting half an hour for the bus, so I got in. It was only when he started rubbing my leg with his left hand I copped on. When he hit the next traffic lights I jumped out.

Years later when I saw the group 'The Village People' I understood the message my lift giver thought he was getting. There were no gays in my village growing up. At least none that I was aware of. And while I can laugh at it now it could have ended up much more serious. Put it like this, I never told my mother or father about it.

During my stay in America, I learned most of all there were many contradictions in being Irish. While half the cops in Boston and New York had roots in the oul' sod, the Irish in the States were tops for breaking the rules.

I saw Irish guys pull just about every stunt imaginable, from using false names to dodging emigration officials and paying zero tax. A lot of the old time Irish bar owners - mainly guys who had emigrated to the States after the Second World War, were up to all sorts of shenanigans. They used to avoid buying from licensed wholesalers where their purchases could be inventoried for tax purposes, by buying crates of cheap booze from the off-licences and then charging full bar prices. And it was common practice – Pete O'Hanlon used to tell me this, and he might have done it himself – for bars to have whiskey bottles with top brand names filled with cheap rye. After a few shots, who could tell whether it was Jameson Special Blend, or a cheap rye bottled in the backroom that morning?

And while we were passionate about discrimination and civil rights at home, at that time some of the most racist and right-wing people I met in the U.S. were Irish. And if it was bad then just look at the number of guys with Irish names on Fox News today spewing out right-wing rubbish.

During several conversations Annie McMenamin's husband, Charlie, told me his stories of how he had emigrated in 1948 to New York. By then he was already in his early 30s but after a couple of tragic deaths in his family from TB, and dispirited by being unable to get steady employment, he thought it best if he, his wife and their young son, Peter, started a new life. It was a huge decision but one that needed to be taken.

A charming, extrovert man Charlie needn't have worried as he made a great success of his life in his adopted country. In fact, he should have been born American. He loved his bow ties, his baseball and his big American cars.

He explained that starting out as a car salesman he was offered a job as manager of a garage but turned it down because he could barely read or write, a fact he hid from the management. He then went into business with his brother as a bartender and eventually owned a very successful bar in Port Washington.

What I found odd was that such a decent man refused to serve black people. I asked him why.

He explained that his bar was where the police and firemen drank after their work and if he started serving blacks, they would take their custom elsewhere. I remember one day a black man came in while I was there, he asked for a beer, and Charlie let on to be getting it for him but left behind the bar and went out to the storeroom where he waited until the guy left.

I really didn't like that.

And I got another example of this kind of approach from Annie. I worked at a Sylvania plant – they made parts for televisions, cameras etc – where one of my colleagues was Bobby Jones, a decent black man.

One night Bobby, who was the night-time supervisor, landed in the worse for wear from something other than alcohol. He could barely move. Part of his function was to go around the building and code in numbers to prove he had checked into the various laboratories where there were strict temperature controls. As I had walked around with Bobby on quite a few occasions I knew the routine and I covered for him.

The next morning as I was standing outside the gate waiting for the bus, Bobby drove up in his huge car insisting no matter where I'm going, he's taking me; I had saved 'his life' because if he lost the job he would be in big trouble. When he took me to Little Neck and dropped me off at Annie's house, she had been standing outside so she wanted to know why a black man had left me home. I told her what had happened, and she suggested I stay away from those 'drug-taking black folks'.

It was a stereotype but that was her world view back then. It was hard to understand why it was so.

Looking back now I have no hesitation in saying that summer changed my life. It was a catalyst. I knew I was never going to be an accountant. Spending my life on picky detail was never going to be my thing; I wanted to live a broad strokes life.

I realised too that not only had I wasted a lot of teachers' time I had wasted a lot of my own, that I was going nowhere because of my lack of focus. Daydreaming about a great future wasn't cutting it in the real world. I came back knowing I needed to find an alternative route out of nowhere, because nowhere was where I was headed.

One other thing was also certain .... I came back very different in terms of personality to the one who had left just short of four months earlier.

I left Ireland in June '72 a relatively quiet person but now back at college I became president of the Students Union, got involved in all aspects of life there and, as a direct result of this involvement, lost the naivety of small-town living. And little did I know that it was all a learning curve for the life that was, eventually, heading my way.

What I, most certainly, never anticipated at that time was that I would eventually become Managing Editor of the largest provincial newspaper group in Ireland or that I would go back to college and earn a Master's degree.

Even in my wildest dreams that would have seemed way too far-fetched.

SNOTTERS, TEA AND NEWS

After studying Business Studies at the Atlantic Technological University in Letterkenny for three years, by some strange meanderings of fate I got a job with the local paper, the Donegal News.

Indeed, had I not had a totally random talk on a Friday afternoon late in April 1974 with a classmate, Gerry Doherty – who I haven't seen in more than half a century – I could have ended up only God knows where.

Gerry was really focused on qualifying as an accountant, and ended up, I am led to believe, with a top job with a big multinational corporation.

But he was approached by a member of ATU staff, Patsy McGonagle, later to manage the Irish team at several Olympics, and asked if he was interested in a job with the Donegal News. Patsy was a weekly contributor to the paper, and had learned that the bosses were on the lookout for a cub reporter. Gerry did not want it, but suggested he knew someone who might – me.

I was the first Editor of the college's student 'magazine' though calling it that is stretching it a bit. The magazine was all of four black and white A4 pages run off by hand on an antiquated Xerox copier at the college which had been discarded by the administrative staff as unfit for use.

Gerry came to me, told me about the reporter job and a kind of interview was set up. Actually it was little more than a conversation. By chance Sean Curran, then in charge of the paper, had seen a copy of the magazine, liked it and offered me a job there and then. All he had to do, he explained, was to clear it with the proprietors back in Omagh. A few days later he got back to me to inform me the job was mine.

It was the most fortuitous stroke of luck in my entire working life.

It is hard to explain in terms of technology these days but back then newspapers were just slightly ahead of smoke signals - no computers, no faxes, no internet, no mobile phones, no broadband, no digital cameras, no Facebook, no Twitter. The height of 'technology' was putting into a manual typewriter a sheet of carbon paper between two A4 size pages and creating a copy.

And the job itself was real grassroots journalism. For the first few years with the Donegal News every Monday I had to go to the Gaeltacht area of west Donegal to do the Cloughaneely and Gweedore notes. This is, almost literally, notes on births, marriages and deaths in the locality. Believe me, this was community journalism in the true sense.

I still vividly recall the very first day I travelled to Gweedore and as I got off the Lough Swilly bus in Bunbeg - it was a beautiful summer's day, probably in early July - a man walking past stating, 'Lá breá anois'.

I replied in English: 'What?'

The village idiot would have known he was saying 'lovely day'.

All those years studying Irish in St. Eunan's really worked for me.

One of the people I called with regularly in Gortahork was Dr. Sean Haughey, the noted folklorist whose book on his father-in-law, Micí Mac Gabhann - *Rotha Mór an tSaoil* – I had studied for the Leaving Cert. It was a widely acclaimed story of Mickey's life, and how the lad who had emigrated in poverty to America, had gone to the Yukon and found gold and was able to come back twenty years later and buy the landlord's big house. It was a much-loved tale.

Sean was an autodidact, a totally self-educated, highly cultured man and a complete gentleman. It was the highlight of my day to hear his stories. And it was an education too.

But I suffered for my craft too. Believe me, I really did. One particularly outstanding memory, for all the wrong reasons, was the day I called into a house in the Falcarragh area where a woman insisted I have a cup of tea. Anyway, as she was lifting down a cup, she sneezed snotters everywhere, cleaned her nose with the tip of her already filthy apron using the exact same spot of the garment where the snotters were still visible to give the cup she was about to put my tea in a wipe. Knowing what was coming, my stomach was churning. When she handed the cup to me, what could I do? I drank it, trying not to puke with every sip.

The best thing by far, however, of that era was that it was probably the last authentic wave of individualism in Irish journalism. Today there is a sort of tunnel all journalists have to go down – secondary school, degree, journalism course. Back in the 1970s it was a lot more freewheeling with a truly eclectic mix of people from all sorts of backgrounds, some with top-of-the-range academic qualifications, others with none. I don't know, either, how some of those old colleagues – all long gone now - would survive in our politically-correct, health and safety conscious days.

Uniformity was not in the dictionary if you wanted a word to describe them. Chain-smoking, coffeeholic Liam Gallagher, of the Donegal Democrat, had been a medical student in Dublin but left after being involved in a serious road crash. He suffered extensive head injuries and lost the ability to do the heavy-duty concentrated study required for medicine. The College of Surgeons' loss was journalism's gain.

He was a total one off with a unique approach to reporting in that he rarely ever had a notebook and was often seen in court taking notes on the back of Major cigarette packets. Despite being a teetotaller and having an 'official' office on Letterkenny's High Road his principal workplace was the Cottage Bar on Main Street where he, quite literally, spent hours drinking cup after cup of coffee while trying to decipher the smallest handwriting in history - his own.

Academically he was a genius. He could quote poetry, speak Latin, play the piano but getting him to sit still for ten minutes could be difficult.

And then there was Willie (Liam) Conaghan, who wrote what was known as the 'Fear Feasa' column for the Derry Journal for more than sixty years yet never, not once, set foot in the paper's headquarters in Derry.

A fastidious little man he was always well organised, and it somehow seemed totally appropriate that on the very day he was buried his last column appeared as usual.

He had one major personality flaw - he was a miser. It's likely he had his Baptism money when he died. His tightness with cash was legendary, even surviving six months of a bank strike without once cashing a single wage cheque. The story goes that when the strike was over, he presented about thirty cheques to the bank manager who was so surprised he rang the Journal to check if they were legitimate. The bank man was perplexed how anyone could survive more than six months seemingly without spending money.

John McIntyre, of the Donegal People's Press, was the reporter's reporter, a man who would disappear for days on end to go playing bridge or off fishing. Then he would work almost 30 hours straight, only napping when the occasion demanded. He was an absolute whirlwind at turning out copy. His typing was on a par with any top secretary in the country and his shorthand was so good he frequently was asked to act as a court stenographer when on occasions the official one didn't show.

While he never got the work-life balance quite right he sure got the life-life balance correct.

However, the man who had the biggest influence was my old boss Sean Curran, one of the most decent people I was to meet in a long career. What you saw was not what you got. Behind a mask of quietness and shyness there resided one of the sharpest, funniest minds imaginable, and I was to prove a massive beneficiary of that in that anything I learned in journalism I learned from him.

He had many qualities and was great at reading people. I recall his great maxim to this day.... the smoother the talker the bigger the con man. It has proved to be almost irrefutable.

The foundation he provided for me allowed me to build a career that has provided a really good life for myself and my family. However, that's not to say it was a lucrative career. Far, far from it. Starting out in local journalism back then included a willingness to accept a living standard just above penury. Owning even the most basic of private vehicles was out of the question for most junior journalists so in a huge county where CIE still does not provide a public bus service a whole different skill set was required when finding innovative solutions to covering news events and fixtures.

For example, when I was told I had to cover Dungloe Court for the first time - an hour away from Letterkenny and over seriously bad, rural mountain roads – I was aware getting there was 'officially' impossible if you had neither a car nor public transport.

The solution? Ring Justice Michael Larkin and get a lift with him. Sure, wasn't it certain the District Judge would be going to the District Court... Get a lift with a judge? Don't think so....

I was wrong. I didn't know Larkin, but John McIntyre did, rang him for me and for about the next five years I used to travel with the good judge to various courts.

It had its moments.

One journey I still laugh about was after a hotly-contested case in Bunbeg and it was clear when we got back into his car at the end of the court, he was obviously annoyed about it, still mulling it over in his mind. He knew he had messed up.

He asked me, 'Pat, what did you think of my decision in that (named) case?'

I, like an idiot, made the mistake of giving him my honest opinion, that he had got it totally wrong. I pointed out that one of the witnesses had totally contradicted the other. It was obvious one of them had told lies.

He didn't speak to me the rest of the way home.

The next time, months later, when he ventured to ask me a similar question I replied, 'Great summation of a very complex case, Judge'. That, apparently, was the right answer.

It was a steep learning curve in the realities of life. And it was great craic.

A STEP UP THE LADDER

I wasn't that long in the game when I, totally unexpectedly, was put in charge of the Donegal News (then titled the Derry People). It was, again, a case of opportunity opening its doors when I least expected it.

As previously mentioned, two major turning points had occurred in Letterkenny which triggered rapid growth. As well as the newly-opened third level college the then giant British textile company, Courtaulds, also announced it was setting up a plant in the town. It promised somewhere in the region of 600 to 700 'well paid industrial jobs'.

These two disparate events proved the catalyst for the birth of a whole new town – new housing estates, new shops and industries, rapid growth in population; the old town almost disappeared overnight.

My boss got caught in the stampede.

Sean Curran owned a stationery store which also doubled up as a toy shop, while out the back of his premises was a small but very busy printing house, the Donegal Printing Company.

The demands of looking after a growing business, a growing family and a growing newspaper took its toll. One night about 3am he fell asleep at his desk, hit his head off the side and gave himself a very nasty cut above the eye. I think that was the final nail in his journalistic career.

His wife, Nora, was rightly concerned about his health so something had to give. He was, almost literally so, killing himself with work.

But before he left, he did me one huge favour.

The owners of the company wanted to bring in an experienced senior journalist, someone to take on an Editor-type role and were going to put an advert in the national papers to see if anyone would take the bait. Sean had another idea. He talked to headquarters in Omagh and on his recommendation I was offered his job, albeit on a trial basis.

And so, at the tender age of 24 - this was early 1978 - I was in charge of my first paper. The short version is that after about three months the 'trial basis' was never mentioned again. I was on my way.

By 1980 there was significant growth. For years Sean had been a one-man band, now I was in charge of a paper with four reporters and a host of correspondents, a full-time photographer plus a couple of freelancers, two advertising representatives and a receptionist. And it was expanding rapidly.

After the pittance I had earned at the outset I was also reasonably well paid, the company even getting me a car. I was, in a way, as snug as a bug in a rug surrounded by family and friends working in the community I had grown up in.

I should have been delighted with myself. But I wasn't.

I didn't know what I wanted but I wanted more than this. It had become predictable, too easy and I was bored.

I came home for lunch on a wet Monday in February 1980 and the wife remarked, 'Did you see the advertisement in yesterday's Sunday Press? RTE are looking for journalists – you should think about applying.'

I paid no attention to the adverts in newspapers – a habit that was to continue throughout my entire career in the newspaper game – and hadn't noticed.

A couple of days later I found myself sending off for application forms to RTE's personnel department on the basis of 'this will be a bit of craic' and thinking to myself that nothing whatever would come of it.

It was, therefore, something of a surprise when I was invited to Dublin about a month later for an interview. I was not at all prepared for that, but we decided, Rosie, my wife and me, that I should go for it. By this stage our rationale was let's see where this takes us. And now the dice was ready to be thrown.

Firstly, all the candidates did something like an IQ test. Then we had to decipher the main points buried in a boring press release and jazz it up. That was part one.

If you got through that, then it was back for a formal interview and then, part three, was a medical to determine whether we were deaf and/or colour blind. It was the former - the hearing thing – that was to prove a wee bit of a problem for me.

Apparently, and I was totally unaware of this, I have hearing like a dog. It was explained to me that the sound test revealed I can hear high pitch and low pitch sounds easily, but the middle range went largely unheard. Little wonder when as a child at Mass and the microphone went to a high pitch whistle I all but jumped out of my seat with a pain in my ear.

The interview was the main component of the entire process. This was the make-or-break part of the deal, the final hurdle.

And a totally strange thing happened on the day I went for that interview.

I decided to go on my own, so I got on the CIE Dublin express from Letterkenny around about 8a.m. Never great first thing in the morning I was half sleeping when I noticed a small man, a Capuchin monk, getting on. There weren't too many passengers, so I was a wee bit surprised when he addressed me saying, 'Mind if I sit beside you and have a chat – I find this long journey unbelievably boring.'

I said not at all and as the hours passed, we talked and debated about the issues of the day. He was a brilliant, interesting man full of fascinating insights.

It was probably somewhere outside of Monaghan when he asked me what I was going to Dublin for, and I responded to him with what I regarded as the honest truth: 'You know, Father,' says I, 'I'm going to Dublin to do an interview for a job as a journalist with RTÉ. I'm probably wasting my time going for it as I haven't a hope in hell of getting it. I have heard there were up to 4,000 applications (there was massive unemployment at this time) so I'm punching way above my weight even to get this interview. I should probably have quit while I was ahead. But I am going to see it through to the end.'

Those were near enough the words I said. It was genuine too, something that I was feeling inside. He stalled for a while before replying and then told me something I have never forgotten.

It went like this: 'Pat, can I tell you something? I figure there are about four percent of the folks in this world who belong in the genius category – the brain surgeons, the rocket scientists – and then there are about four percent who are intellectually disabled or challenged or whatever it's called these days. In my opinion there's very little we can do about either of these groups, so we'll leave them aside.

'So, that leaves at least 90% percent of us who are just as capable as each other. You are approaching this interview in the wrong frame of mind. I would suggest you are as good as the next man. I have talked to you for a couple of hours now and I can tell you are every bit as bright and as intelligent as the people who will be asking you the questions in a couple of hours' time.'

It was just what I needed to hear.

I never met that monk again.

I don't know his name, don't know why he was on the bus that day, or why he decided to chat to me; he had the choice of about forty other seats to go sit in. But I have remembered his words almost verbatim to this day.

In fact, I have often used his advice when dealing with young people in the same situation now as I was then. While I don't know if it was God's plan – some folk I have told this story to suggest that it was! It certainly calmed me, and it gave me just the sort of attitude I needed when I went into the interview with a group of heavyweight RTE types including Rory O'Connor, Head of

Television, and Barney Cavanagh, News Editor. I had decided, like my monk friend had suggested, not to be nervous but to go with the flow.

It must have worked because despite the fact it was a very tough interview I was offered a job just about a week later.

The day the letter arrived I didn't know whether to laugh or cry. Believe it or not, the complicated bit was being married and having a family. Had I been single it wouldn't have been an issue.

Shortly after we got married Rosie and I figured out the only way we could afford our own home was to give up renting and buy a mobile home which we sited in my parents back garden. As a result of living there for well over a year my father and mother had become very attached to our children. And our children were seriously attached to them. That was a problem. We also had a big network of family and friends, people whom we visited and socialised with. Now we were going off to Dublin where we knew no one and no one knew us.

It seems pathetic now, but it was a massively big decision for us to leave all this behind.

This was the era where there were no mobile phones, no email – indeed there wasn't even a landline in the house we had rented in the capital - and 'The Troubles' in the north meant that going to and from Dublin was neither pleasant nor particularly safe. There had been numerous stories of cars with southern registrations getting attacked by stone throwers and hostile gestures in some hard-line unionists' towns were not uncommon. The roads were atrocious too so getting from north Donegal was well over four hours travel.

But after a lot of deliberation on the pros and cons of the move, what swung the decision in favour of taking the job was that it was a step forward, going from a provincial paper to the national broadcaster. It was time to spread my wings.

DUBLIN DAYS, SHORT STAY

The very first morning I went into RTE - it was a Monday - I was called in by Barney Cavanagh, the News Editor, to be asked how I fancied a trip to Donegal? What?

It could only happen to me... 'But I have only just arrived from Donegal,' says I, somewhat confusedly

Being so busy moving house and home that weekend I hadn't heard the news that the Ceann Comhairle, Fianna Fail's Joe Brennan, had died in his native Bruckless in South Donegal, and as there was a fair bit of political turmoil at the time, it was decided by the newsroom that they should have their own man to cover the funeral.

I had to go back to the house we had moved into a little over twelve hours earlier. To make matters worse Rosie wasn't there; she had taken the kids out for a walk. So, rather than giving her the option of coming with me or staying, all I could do was leave her a note telling her I was away back to Donegal.

Needless to say, that was a traumatic beginning for life in Dublin for Rosie, just 23-years-old, sitting in a house where the furniture still hadn't arrived, where there was no phone and where she was on her own with two young children. She, needless to say, felt totally isolated and vulnerable. She didn't sleep a wink, she later told me, for two nights and every strange noise caused panic. With the crime rate and drug problem rapidly rising in that area of Dublin at that time, she had every reason to be nervous.

But that sojourn back to Donegal got my short RTE career off to a flying start.

I was to spend just over a year there and I did enjoy it. I spent a lot of time in the Political Unit with Sean Duignan, RTE's Political Editor, who was a genuinely lovely fella, and his deputy, fellow Donegal man, Donal Kelly, who later succeeded Duignan.

It really was a hugely important time in that there were three General Elections in about eighteen months as Charlie Haughey and Garret FitzGerald battled it out for supremacy. Neither of them could get the electorate to give them an overall mandate.

I was not sure, however, that broadcasting was the medium for me.

I had earlier done a camera test which was so awful they decided not to put me in front of the camera but to play to my strengths as a reporter-cum-sub-editor. I loved this kind of work so maybe a national newspaper would have been a more natural move, but I hadn't thought that through.

My one major claim to fame during my RTE career is that I was the 'early' sub on the news desk the day John Lennon was shot. So, the words read that morning informing the Irish public of the momentous news that the former Beatle had been murdered were mine.

I was also heavily involved in the 'Stardust' fire coverage in that Barney Cavanagh told me to keep on top of all the various reports coming in and to write overall intros for the newsreaders. This was an awful tragedy, hundreds of young people in a Dublin nightclub caught in a fire-trap building in which many of them died. One of the cameramen sent out to cover the story was later to learn that his daughter had a lucky escape. She had been in the ballroom but had left for some reason. But while he was covering the fire, he had no idea where his daughter was. He told me that they were the worst hours of his life.

Things were going so well that after about nine or ten months Barney approached me again suggesting I go for the job as Chief Sub-Editor for the Dail output. This would mean I would be responsible for all copy – not broadcasting - and where the salary would be that of a chief sub in the newsroom which was pretty good. The guy in position was, he explained, coming up to retirement and they wanted a safe pair of hands. He suggested I keep it in mind. I told him I would.

I got talking to one of the chief subs who I had become friendly with, and he disclosed the salary of an RTE chief sub. Considering what I had been used to living on moneywise, this would be a significant improvement. He too had come from a provincial paper and was of the opinion this was a good move. I was all but convinced by these arguments and had settled myself down to do Dublin as a long-haul stay.

But the best-laid plans don't factor in fate.

Just a little over a year into the job we came home to Donegal on a break. My wife insisted one function we had to attend was her aunt and uncle's 50th wedding anniversary party in Carndonagh. I was reluctant to go but in her eyes, it was not up for discussion. So, off we went.

I was sitting having a drink when Larry Doherty walked in. You always knew when Larry made an entrance as he was like the Pope in the northwest region – everyone knew him, and he knew most of them.

While officially the Derry Journal's chief photographer, he had covered the Troubles for many of the big international media outlets and national papers, having photographs published regularly in the early days in prestigious magazines like 'Time' and 'Newsweek'. And modesty and quietness were not Larry's strong suits So, to repeat, when he walked into a room, everyone knew he was there.

I too had known him before this event as we had met at several functions, but we were not particularly well acquainted. However, during the evening he made a point of coming over to me and asking how I was liking Dublin. I told him that I could only quote Austin Hunter, an old friend from the BBC, staunch unionist and a 'good Prod' – his own words – that 'they (the Southerners) were not like us Northerners'. Which was certainly true back then.

Larry soon had a suggestion. If I was interested, he was certain there was a job going as Chief Reporter with the Derry Journal but, he explained, the real carrot was that it was a bit of a ruse - they were actually looking for an Editor. The current Editor was, if I was picking up the vibe correctly, showing outward signs of being unhappy with the job. Would I be interested?

I don't think I answered the question and what happened next is somewhat confusing, but I think the sequence of events was that an advertisement for a Chief Reporter appeared in the 'Journal' and Larry then rang me to tell me about it. I didn't fill in any forms but sent a letter of interest to the 'Journal' thinking little about what I was really doing. The only bit I'm now certain of is that I recall one of the staff in the Dail coming on to the press gallery, tapping me on the shoulder and saying there is 'a fella, Colm McCarroll of the Derry Journal on the line looking for you in the press office'.

Apparently, Colm had tried RTE's newsroom, looked up the phone directory for a home phone but couldn't find one so had no method of contact. It was only the kindness of someone in RTE who suggested he ring the Press Gallery in the Dail.

The fact that he had been so persistent indicated to me he was not messing about, that he was very interested in what I had to offer. He suggested the next time I was up home I should give him a shout in Derry, adding that he preferred that I make it sooner rather than later. About two weeks later I met him.

He told me at the outset the job was mine but there was no way he could pay me what RTE was. But he sold a good story. He pointed out that living in Northern Ireland was about 25 per cent cheaper than the Republic and that what I would lose one way I would make up the other. I could get a better house and at a very much better price in Derry than in Dublin. That wasn't totally true, but it wasn't that far off the mark either as we did, eventually, get a five-bedroom house in the Culmore area that still remains the warmest, most snug house we have ever lived in.

But that was in the future, there was one more immediate major hurdle to overcome.

Here I was working for RTE, the boy from the small town who, despite the inauspicious start, had done quite well for himself. How would my parents react to me leaving a prestigious job with the national broadcaster to go to a city where there were bombings and shootings and where the Hunger Strikes had polarised the community to unprecedented levels? This was something that did concern me.

In terms of pros and cons my parents made it clear they saw few of the former and a hell of a lot of the latter in moving to Derry. They had a point, of that there was no doubt.

My prospects in RTE were quite good too, or least that's what I was being led to believe. Now there was a big decision to make again. What was the right decision?

Mentally, I began doing the old 'pros' versus 'cons' routine for myself.

I was a country boy used to wide open spaces and mountains and rivers. I hated being hemmed in, and I was finding the constant traffic congestion in Dublin almost claustrophobic. Drugs were also starting to appear big time with heroin then freely available. Crime was notably on the increase, quite a few houses around where we lived in Ballinteer being broken into. I also had two young children, one ready to start school so if I was going to move, better do it before we got locked into schools etc. Amazing too the extraneous things that go through your head. In Donegal, being able to go to the pub with your real friends, people saying hello to you on the street, being able to go for a walk in a forest or on a wide-open empty beach were important to me. They all came into play. I missed all that.

I waited for about a week, discussed it with Rosie and we finally decided that 'going home' had more pluses than minuses for us. Thus, my short career as a national broadcaster – who never did broadcast during that period – was over.

MURDERS AND INFORMERS

Bishop Daly used to make all his major statements on Mondays and Thursdays to ensure coverage in the next day's Derry Journal. It was a good strategy. I never discussed it with him directly though I would presume he knew it only too well that the IRA used to do the same.

At its peak with circulation twice a week of approximately 26,000 to 30,000 copies per publication (from about 1985 to 2005), statistics from back then would indicate that each newspaper was read by an average of at least six people. That meant each edition was read by, possibly, up to 130,000 people.

The Journal was bought by just about every Catholic/nationalist family in most of the northern half of the huge Catholic diocese of Derry, and also circulated widely in the Inishowen peninsula in north Donegal.

In terms of media penetration, it was unrivalled.

The Troubles were confined to only six counties, so this one paper spoke to a considerable number of the very people the nationalist leaders, in particular, really wanted to talk to.

Derry was at the epicentre, the heartland of this conflict and it's not an exaggeration to state that all sides were interested in getting their views to the hearts and minds of that Journal readership. The battle for hearts and minds really was fiercely contested. And it was relentless as the violence was in full flow.

One incident I recall particularly well for a lot of the wrong reasons was that while off on a week's break in the early 1990s I met a Journal staffer (now deceased) on a Thursday afternoon in Shipquay Street. With hundreds streaming by we had a quick chat, and I knew something was up.

I could tell by his body language something big was going down. He was fidgety, nervous and anxious to get going, not his usual, prevaricating 'let's go for a cup of coffee' type self.

So, when I confronted him with a straight question, out it came: 'They are going to shoot someone ...they have found out he's an informer.'

And with that he walked away.

I didn't solicit any details, nor did he offer any. Sure enough the next day's lead story confirmed that the IRA had shot dead a young fella late on Thursday night.

At a time of mayhem this death would have gone down as just another violent incident in a long line of violent incidents.

There was so much going on at this time I had adopted an almost detached approach. As Editor, I had a job to do, and this was nothing personal. I wasn't, I reasoned, responsible for what the IRA did, or was doing.

What made this one different was his mother came to see me about ten days after his killing. It was very personal to her. And as she came into the office, I knew this was not a polite social call. I recall a woman whose torment etched on her face was raw and to me, on first impression, she looked like she was dying from the inside out. And her visceral pain was obvious from the outset.

I tried to offer my condolences on the loss of her son but she was having none of it.

Her first comments were, basically, this: 'My son was shot on Thursday so his death could be a big headline in your paper – you are all disgusting.'

In the statement the Journal had obtained in regard to the execution of this young lad, the IRA said he was a member and had been acting as an RUC informer for almost four years, and had been receiving regular payments.

Clearly the central thrust of her argument was right. The Journal did know what was going down before it actually happened. We might not have known the details – the name, where he was being held, when he was going to be shot – but we did know that it was going to happen.

The young lad was shot dead as an example to others, and the IRA was sending a message to anyone they considered an informer. We were the messenger. That was the reality.

Almost a year earlier I had had another encounter with a parent destroyed by the death of a child – also labelled an informer.

I used to try to get to a gym at lunch time just to take my brain to a different place. I knew one of the regulars there. I used to meet him two or three times a week and we would acknowledge each other with a few pleasantries. This particular day turned out to be very different.

'Hey Pat,' said this man with an intensity in his eyes that blazed, 'would you put in that paper of yours that I want to go to Hell to meet the bastards who murdered my son. That's where them fuckers are going.....'

I was aware that I hadn't seen him for some months so was genuinely stunned not only by the unexpectedness of the comment but by the vehemence of the words.

At the time of this conversation, I had no idea it was his son's body that had been discovered on a lonely border road.

There were numerous allegations floating about at the time. One was that he had been deliberately sacrificed to protect a higher-up informant in the IRA. This came into the rumour mill after it was alleged a document was deliberately left lying on a courtroom table some months earlier where it could be seen by a number of republicans who were appearing in court. In that document there was enough innuendo or evidence – I am not sure which - to suggest that they had a mole inside an IRA Active Service unit and that a number of IRA actions had been sabotaged on instructions from his handlers.

Whatever the truth or whether this was black propaganda so that an innocent man could be deliberately sacrificed to protect a higher-up informer we'll never know.

One thing that was patently clear is that his family certainly didn't believe he was guilty of informing on anyone.

My initial introduction to this real-life world of up-close violence was rough and traumatic. It was early in my editorial career when the IRA 'used' – please note the inverted commas here - the Journal to justify the shooting dead of a young Derry man. It was the usual routine so I didn't pay any particular attention – a Thursday when we were asked to send a reporter up to a press conference where the local Sinn Fein office told us a young fella would admit to informing.

The press conference usually consisted of few members of the local press, namely a Derry Journal reporter and a photographer and if the local radio station, Radio Foyle had somebody spare they might come along too. If the Irish News and Belfast Telegraph had somebody available – they had satellite staff in Derry – they, on occasions, would come along.

This time Siobhan Quinn reported and was sent with a photogrpaher to cover the conference and came back with a story and pics. In her story Siobhan told how a married man with three kids had allegedly 'supplied information' to the security services for three years.

Back then the usual modus operandi in dealing with informers was that if the alleged guilty party would admit guilt publicly, he (it was always a he) would be put out of town with a warning never to come back. This one proved different.

My family and I used to go up to my parents' house in Letterkenny to spend part of the weekend – in that pre mobile phone era, the newsroom always knew where I would be – so in the early hours of Sunday morning I got a call from a quite distraught Siobhan telling me that the man had been shot dead by the IRA as an informer.

She had, she told me, just learned his body had been found not far from her own family home. She was really, really upset, claiming we had been used to justify a murder of a young family man.

What was worse was that not only did she know this man and his family but that that particular day she had been the only reporter at the press conference.

The outing of so-called informers was so regular then that it was hardly news. Had the other news organisations reported it she wouldn't have felt so isolated.

And the sickening feeling that had been at the pit of my stomach didn't get any better as the day wore on with the front page of the Derry Journal being used in all the broadcast media coverage. Indeed, ITN's national news gave real prominence to the Journal's front page to explain the 'savagery and brutality' of the guerrilla war that was being fought on the streets of 'a British city.'

I knew we had been used, and I raged internally that I had behaved so naively as an Editor. We had definitely been used by the Republican Movement to justify publicly what, I believe, they had always planned to do privately – shoot the man dead.

In the coming days I made my views known to various republicans that we would never again be party to a press conference like that. We were not going to be used to justify executions.

It might need a highly qualified anthropologist or some sort of behavioural psychologist to explain it all but to my mind it could be argued the Troubles totally skewed all normal societal values and reactions.

From my position in the Editor's Chair in the Derry Journal back then Derry came across more like the wild west than a society where the rule of law and order was adhered to.

It's not an original thesis; many people, academics and such, have put it forward to explain the disintegration of the norms that had held most communities together.

I had personal experience to corroborate the authenticity of my particular thesis, that the law of the jungle had precedence. One story in particular is a prime example.

In December 1992 I was told there were two people at reception who had asked to speak to me specifically. They would not, said the receptionist who put the call through, talk to a reporter. 'Send them in' was my response.

In came a young couple both of whom were clearly agitated, nervous and upset.

It turned out their eldest child, a daughter aged ten, had been sexually abused and, over the next couple of hours, they told their story giving graphic details of what had been done to her. It was way at the worst end of the sexual abuse scale. And they were in a total bind in regard to what they could do about it.

Because of the Troubles there were all kinds of communal prohibitions in place. Had they called in the hated RUC to investigate they would have been ostracised. Not that the people would have objected to abuse of children being investigated, but the reality was that the RUC used every legitimate situation, every interaction with the Catholic community to inveigle themselves into people's lives. Their clear intent was, in the eyes of most nationalists, not to be a normal police force going about its job without fear or favour but of obtaining information on republicans.

So, calling in the RUC ... that wasn't an option.

They told too of how they had tried the low-profile approach by getting in touch with Social Services but little or nothing by way of counselling had been provided for their daughter who was, they said, showing increasing signs of trauma and psychological disturbance. Unlike now there seemed to be little awareness then of the magnitude of the abuse problem. They had, they said, talked to social workers but, apparently, one day when they were out someone had visited, didn't find them at home and after sticking a few leaflets through their letterbox walked away never to be heard of again.

Every avenue they went down was a dead end. As their situation was rapidly deteriorating and as they couldn't get help or justice for their daughter or themselves, they decided to go public.

At the end of their tether, they decided to come to the Journal as they wanted publicity to push someone, somewhere in authority, to come to their aid before they had a tragedy on their hands.

It was an explosive story. A pandora's box was suddenly opened.

In their interview they made clear that apart from telling of their own personal anguish they wanted it to be put out publicly that they were aware from what their daughter had told them that there had been widespread abuse going on in the area for some time and that there were a lot of other victims, as their daughter had named other children she had seen in the perpetrator's house. They assumed that many of the parents of these children were unaware of what was happening. Or, if they were aware, they were burying their heads in the sand not wishing to publicly acknowledge the 'shame' of having a child as a sex abuse victim

I did the story and it appeared as the lead on the Friday edition in early December. The reaction came two days later when IRA men smashed down the door of a local man, an unemployed labourer, and shot him in both legs using a heavy-duty firearm. What happened next is unclear. Whether the people in the area never heard this man calling for help or they did and chose to ignore his appeals has never been established, but by the time the ambulance arrived almost all the blood in his body had gone.

On the way to Altnagelvin Hospital his heart stopped, and both his legs were so damaged they had to be amputated later the same day. The medical intervention was to no avail, he died the next day.

There was a mixed reaction to our story.

While the vast majority saw it as straight-forward reporting, some people tried to suggest that our story had led to vigilantism, that we had somehow encouraged people to take the law into their own hands.

In my opinion, that was absolutely wrong.

Our article was totally legitimate, a straightforward story about a family claiming there was widespread abuse in a large estate in Derry city – and nothing was being done about it.

There was no way to sanitise or make it palatable; it was what it was. Over the years there have been hundreds of similar stories in papers on the island of Ireland, the only difference was the reaction because of the political situation in that place at that time.

It was simple if looked at straightforwardly. We were in the middle of the longest running urban war in the world where normal laws and rules did not apply. It was not Dublin 4 or the leafy suburbs of Cheshire. Derry was not, to quote Mrs Thatcher, as British as Finchley.

The story related earlier in this chapter in regard to the now-deceased Journal staffer is a clear case in point. With the benefit of the long lens of hindsight, some might suggest he should have contacted the police and a life might have been saved. The reality was the staffer's life expectancy in such a situation would have been extremely limited – and the alleged informer would still have been shot. That's not supposition, it would have been fact. The IRA would have seen both as informers. It was an era of journalism where the choice was often between rocks and hard places.

GARRET'S HISTORIC VISIT

For many years I was an ardent jogger. I tried to get out at least once a day. Even when I was working late I would often jog from the Journal office out to our home in Culmore – about five or six miles – just to get my head cleared. But even then there could be no getting away from life as the Editor.

On Monday night I had barely reached home and was having a quick shower before heading back in when I heard a big commotion in our hallway.

'Where is he? Where is he? I need to talk to him urgently.' Or words to that effect.

It was Larry Doherty and he was in a real tizzy. When a man who has been chief photographer at the paper for years and has been to the forefront of riots and civil unrest is so excited, I knew there was something big going down.

Out I come and Larry is so full of excitement he can hardly get the words out.... 'Hume was down looking for you. He wants to talk to you urgently. Garret FitzGerald is coming to Derry tomorrow and he's bringing a whole lot of big nobs with him. And they want to come to the Journal. You had better ring him.'

The one small problem was that this was the era before mobile phones so I had to get back to the office and then spend half the time trying to edit the next morning's edition and the other half trying to find Hume who was also up to his eyeballs preparing for the FitzGerald visit.

It was madness for a couple of hours in that all I had were second-hand details about a major event where we were going to be centre stage. And the advance notice, for obvious security reasons, was tight to put it mildly.

FitzGerald's visit was a big deal. This was big news on every level. Symbolically it was massive.

The first and only time a serving Taoiseach had visited the North previously was the catalyst for bringing an end to the career of the Prime Minister, Terence O'Neill. The visit of Sean Lemass had brought protests on to the streets led by an emerging demagogue, Ian Richard Kyle Paisley. There hadn't been one since, and twenty years had passed.

For years unionism had attempted to portray the border between Northern Ireland and the Republic as if it were the Atlantic Ocean, impenetrable, a fortress against the rebels who would invade from the South. That FitzGerald was making a political statement by heading North was seriously significant.

In the background to the visit, major negotiations were ongoing between the British and Irish governments on what was to become known as the Anglo-Irish Agreement. It was to prove both a highly-controversial agreement and historically of major importance.

British prime minister Margaret Thatcher almost had to be dragged kicking and screaming to sign it in late November 1985. She did so at the insistence of her cabinet colleagues and her senior civil servants.

To the absolute outrage of the unionist community, it gave the Dublin government an 'advisory role' in the affairs of the North. That doesn't sound like much but in terms of the symbolism it was mighty important.

It would seem FitzGerald, aware of where the talks were at, was sending his own signal that times were changing when he arrived in Derry that morning in early 1985. His entourage included the Minister for Foreign Affairs, Peter Barry, and a large cohort of officials and diplomats including Sean Donlon, later to be Secretary General of the Department of Foreign Affairs, and a Derry man, Jim Sharkey, later to be one of Ireland's most respected ambassadors.

Indeed, while he has never confirmed it, I suspect that Sharkey had been a key influencer in selecting his hometown as the chosen location for the visit.

That morning there was fervid activity at the Journal as attempts were made to give the place a quick clean up. Of course, being a printing facility with paper everywhere that was impossible. My wife insisted that the day was of such importance, I forwent my traditional ensemble of tank top and trousers and don a suit. Typical Derry Journal. I arrived to a chorus of 'ooh, look at him'.

I was hardly seated in my chair when the receptionist told me there were RUC men at the desk and they wanted to do what they called 'a sweep of the building'. There were other armed officers standing guard outside.

In they came with a couple of sniffer dogs, did a quick recce and out again.

Then a fleet of cars drove in and out we went, Frank McCarroll Snr, Managing Director, Colm McCarroll, General Manager, and myself, the Editor, to meet our guests.

FitzGerald turned out to be a charming man, much more attuned to what was going on than his somewhat intellectual/academic persona suggested. He knew, or was well briefed, about local issues and local personalities.

Peter Barry had the urbane approach of a well-educated rich man which was a reflection of exactly what he was. He was one of the 'Princes of Cork', a member of the Barry's Tea empire.

From the general conversation it emerged very clearly that events in the North were impacting massively on the political and economic life of the South. The Taoiseach and the Minister for Foreign Affairs were, obviously, trying to ameliorate that. Finding a solution that the nationalist people would find acceptable was key to progress down that track.

What was very clear was these were baby steps for the Dublin government in terms of official engagement in the North. What had been referred to previously as 'megaphone diplomacy' was to be replaced by a formalised agreement where the southern government members and officials could have direct access to British ministers and civil servants to make their views known at official level.

I learned a lot of what was going on in the background that day. I had a quick conversation with Sean Donlon and was impressed. He was both an intelligent man and a smart man, two very different things. He had a breadth of knowledge but also had emotional intelligence in that he had the ability to get onto the wavelength of the person he was talking to.

And he used a phrase that day I heard for the first time but have heard a million times since.

Referring to the torturous negotiations that were said to be nearing conclusion I asked him if there would be a deal. I recall him stating that about ninety-five per cent was agreed but 'nothing is agreed until everything is agreed.' Now there's a phrase for the ages.

Once the formal part was over, we were all invited over to the Everglades Hotel for a big slap-up meal. All the usual suspects were there, the great and the good of the city, and a couple of major Fine Gael figures from across the Border in Donegal.

The Irish delegation, in particular, was in great good humour. The visit had gone so much better than even they expected. FitzGerald had visited several places, had met with representatives of the local community including members of unionist civic society and had been received courteously. There had been no public protests and the extensive media coverage had been positive.

For me, it was one of those days I realised was historic, that instinct told me the ground was shifting, the old certainties no longer certain.

One little rider to this worth recounting is that in the summer of 1986, the deputy leader of the SDLP, Seamus Mallon, called in and we got into conversation about the Anglo-Irish Agreement. During our discussion I admitted to being more than a little underwhelmed by it, that we're all supposed to jump with hands in the air in triumph at Dublin getting the opportunity to have 'an advisory role' in the North? After all the death, mayhem and suffering was that it? I suggested the analogy of an ashtray on a motorbike.

To my surprise Mallon not only laughed but agreed.

But then he made the salient point that while nationalism might not have seen it as any wonderful achievement, but for unionism it was something they would have to face. For him, he said, it was akin to someone putting a nail hole close to the top of a water bucket. Originally, it's thought to be no big deal but once the hole was there, water would escape, and the hole would eventually get bigger as time wore on.

What he was suggesting was that nationalists should have patience, that unionism's total control was now breached, albeit only slightly. But it was a start, something to be built on.

I would think most unionists would see his analogy as prophetic. He was a wise man, was Seamus!

DALY'S DOSE OF REALISM

Bishop Edward Daly was a bit of an outsider in Derry in that he wasn't a native of the city. He was born, like me, in Donegal and brought up in the border village of Belleek in Co. Fermanagh. As a young lad his parents, who were shopkeepers, raised enough money to send him as a boarder to St Columb's and that was the start of his long association with the Derry diocese. After his secondary education he opted for the priesthood and studied for five years in Rome.

Post ordination, he served in Co. Tyrone, then moved to Derry and later worked for a time, again like myself, in RTE. And his role during Bloody Sunday was to bring him to international attention as the priest waving the white hankie in the iconic photo.

Like Hume, he could be a very different person in private than when public facing. It took me a while to understand this but once I did, he became a friend, someone I liked greatly. And the best bit of advice I got during my years as Editor I got from him.

I wasn't long in the job when I was invited to a private dinner by some organisation or other. It totally escapes me now. I recall I was sitting with him, Ian Kennedy, the Head of the still relatively-new BBC Radio Foyle, and a number of others.

Like a lot of people brought up in the South I had a somewhat naive viewpoint, a sort of black and white opinion of what was wrong and what was right. During the discussion around the table that afternoon I expounded on my views, stating with somewhat censorious righteousness that those who engaged in violence were wrong. There were no excuses, no ifs and buts.

When the function was ending Bishop Daly sidled up to me and said: 'Pat, have you got five minutes? I have a wee bit of advice that I would like to share with you.'

Over the next half an hour he told me that he wasn't disagreeing with the overall concept of what I was saying but I should be a little less strident in my condemnation. He pointed out that we all needed to 'walk in the shoes' of those who had felt they had no recourse but to use violence. The question was - what made them decide to do so?

And he asked, was there a concept of a just war? How often should someone be expected to turn the other cheek? Was sectarianism, bigotry and discrimination over fifty plus years enough to justify violence to overturn those injustices?

He made it clear that morality said that we should not kill or use violence but that human beings were not robots, that anger, hatred and hurt could release strong reactions in what were otherwise totally decent people. He had, he said, met IRA activists and supporters who, had they lived in another time and place, could, he believed, have led blameless lives.

I remember we got into a whole discussion of whether, for example, a German had sacrificed himself in assassinating Hitler – would that person sit at the right hand of God for his heroic sacrifice to save others, or would he be in Hell for committing murder.

'Judge not, that ye be not judged,' as the bible says. That was what he was trying to tell me.

BISHOP HEGARTY AND ME!

I got a call from Bishop Daly in early 1993 asking me to call up to his headquarters at St Eugene's Cathedral. It was an unusual request in that most times when he had something to say he just rang, and we talked about what was bothering him over the phone. So, as he rarely asked for anything, off I went.

When I entered his office, I could see immediately that he wasn't well. Some years earlier he had a stroke, and this had affected both his speech and his mobility. Indeed, he had told me that because of the effects of the stroke he arranged most of his public works for the mornings because as the day progressed both his ability to talk clearly and move easily declined rapidly.

I had talked to him regularly, but I was surprised at how tired he looked in the flesh.

After offering me a cup of coffee he came straight to the point – he was resigning from the bishopric. He was simply no longer able to meet the demands of the role either physically or mentally. I was genuinely shocked and surprised at his announcement, but I had physical evidence right in front of me to understand why he was doing it.

After extending my good wishes on his impending retirement and thanking him for his great help over the years, I asked him what happened now? He replied that he had already formally sent a letter of resignation to Rome and that that had been accepted. So, the search for his successor was underway.

It took the best part of a year before that announcement came, and when it came it was a bit of a shock. His successor was to be the incumbent of the Raphoe Diocese, Bishop Seamus Hegarty. And it was a shock to many clergy in the Derry diocese and, I believe, a cause of some resentment amongst some at least.

The feeling was that many good and well-able people had been passed over by the conservative faction of the Catholic Church both in Ireland and further afield. It was suggested at the time, and I don't have any proof whatever that this was so, that the Papal Nuncio in Dublin had urged his bosses back in Rome to go for an old-style conservative.

If this advice was the deciding factor, then they most certainly did. Seamus Hegarty, bishop in the neighbouring diocese, was the shock announcement as Daly's successor. He was to the right on just about every issue, opposing all attempts to liberalise the church's stance on issues such as divorce and abortion.

I got a call from the Irish Times asking me to write an opinion piece on the appointment. I agreed. In the article I laid it on the line stating the incoming bishop would have big shoes to fill, that he was replacing a legend. I also stated that there were rumblings within the clergy in the Derry Diocese that one of their number had been passed over, the implication being that none of them was worthy of promotion.

I also pointed out that Hegarty's reputation was that of an arch-conservative and that could pose difficulties too in Derry where the Troubles had required a lot of priests to elasticate their priestly attitudes to fit in with the realities of everyday living in a society in conflict.

But one major error occurred in the article that was published, and it was definitely not of my making.

In the article I stated very clearly that Hegarty was an experienced pair of hands taking over at a difficult time. That he was highly academic and well able for the job, that he would certainly get the support of the traditional Catholic community. This very important paragraph was omitted from the article which appeared in the Irish Times which came across as almost entirely negative, and Hegarty never forgave me for it.

I never once got a call from him or was asked to meet him. Of course, I never rang him either.

At the behest of a friend of his, a Donegal priest who was also a friend of mine, I was asked to write a letter explaining what had happened. I was reluctant to do so in that I believed when you are explaining you are losing but after more urging I did so.

In the letter I explained what had happened. I also stated that a senior member of the Irish Times who had commissioned the article - she had actually phoned me on the Saturday morning the article appeared to apologise - was willing to state that a sub-editor had excised the paragraph in question not out of malice but simply to get the article to fit the allotted space.

I got a letter back some weeks later which I think reflected Hegarty's personality. It was far from gracious and basically saying he bagged the explanation-cum-apology but that he wouldn't be reaching out any time soon. His response made me regret writing my letter in the first place.

That letter from Hegarty is in my house somewhere, but I cannot find it.

Despite never once having a conversation with him or really meeting him I had a bit of history with Hegarty. In his early days in the priesthood, he had been Principal of Cloughaneely Community School based in Falcarragh, in west Donegal. It tells you a lot about his character that he was nicknamed by his pupils as 'The Bull'. He was big into physical punishment.

It got so bad that one day I got a call from a surprising source, a well-respected Fianna Fail public representative, who told me that if he got one more complaint about pupils being physically abused at the school, he would be going public with it. He asked would I be willing to run with it. Like any journalist worth his salt, I told him I would be more than willing.

I don't know if this person went back to Fr. Hegarty, as he was then, and told him of our conversation. Maybe he did, maybe he didn't. All I do know is that the public representative concerned never did come back to me. If he did make it clear he would go to the media and had made that known to the school boss, I presume the new Bishop of Derry already knew who I was.

The only up-side to emerge from the Irish Times article was when Bishop Daly rang. He said he hadn't been feeling great on the day the article came out but when he read what I had said about him that it had cheered him up immensely. I was glad at least he got to see that.

And one really funny thing about this whole episode occurred several years later.

Martin McGuinness and Bishop Hegarty were avid fishermen, men who would rather go out to a river and spend hours than do almost anything else. I don't know how they became friends in that Hegarty was certainly no republican, well certainly not to my knowledge. But fish together they did and, by all accounts, very regularly.

I remember getting a call from Martin: 'Pat, are you in the office? I'll give you a shout in 15 minutes.'

It was, again, unusual so I thought I was getting some big political exclusive. In walks Martin and I ask him what's up:

'Bishop Hegarty doesn't like you,' says he with a look of concern on his face.

'Jeez, Martin,' says I, in bitter disappointment, 'tell me something I don't know.'

AND THE GOOD GUYS WERE?

For years the establishments in both Ireland and Britain have liked to promote the paradigm that there was a clear delineation between the good guys and the bad guys. And for years this was the version bought by so many who read newspapers like the Sunday Independent and believed some of the more right-wing columnists in the Irish and British media.

It's a paradigm I have difficulty accepting as being a true reflection of the conflict as I came to see it. The reality is there were few players during the Troubles who could claim to have clean hands. It was a dirty game in that the establishment – the courts, the police and security service - were all up to their eyeballs in dirty deeds. And anyone who suggests differently is either naïve or doesn't know what they are talking about.

Whilst the propaganda machine of the time liked to portray the State and the security forces as the good guys, the honest brokers caught in the middle of two warring factions, there is now incontrovertible evidence to the contrary.

In fact, there was incontrovertible evidence years back in the day but, as it didn't suit the narrative of the time, much of it was suppressed. The Dublin government, as we know now, had plenty of evidence to know better.

In the North the RUC and the British security services were active players on the side of unionism and loyalism. The evidence collated by various sources is, as I said, incontrovertible.

Even from the off it was acknowledged that British operations such as internment were partisan. And many of the people detained illegally at that time were ill-treated to the point that the use of the term torture would be legitimate. Semantics in regard to the legal definition of torture doesn't change the reality of what they had to endure.

There are any number too of first-hand accounts of people arrested being seriously manhandled by both the British army and the RUC. Courts jailed people on often risible evidence. Pro-unionist judges often made comments to nationalists appearing before them which clearly exposed their bias.

Talk to any of the more senior solicitors in places like Derry and they can give chapter and verse of decisions that were unsustainable based on the evidence presented.

Whether or not someone before the court is innocent or guilty, a truly impartial judge makes a decision on the evidence before the court, not on his/her bias. That lack of impartiality, that bias was often on full view.

Much more insidious was the use of black propaganda.

One particular area where it was used widespread was in relation to people released without charge. This should have been a clean sheet for most people in a normal society. But in the North it rarely was. When they went back to their communities the security services would often leak claims that the only reason they had got off was that they had named names. That was why so-and-so was arrested the previous night.

It was part of what was known as 'black-ops', part of the British dirty war as espoused by General Sir Frank Kitson. It was done deliberately to plant confusion and suspicion.

It was particularly nasty in small, tight-knit neighbourhoods. For years many totally innocent people had had to live with allegations they were touts, something that would be akin to being accused of paedophilia in a community today. It destroyed many lives.

There were also many vulnerable young people who were actually recruited under duress, paid monies to inform and, once they lost their usefulness, were thrown to the wolves.

People hiding the fact they were gay, or bisexual were particularly vulnerable to blackmail. This, in a conservative society, was a no-no so they were often targeted.

One particular informer who gave the names of numerous alleged IRA men was said to have been compromised after he had a one-night stand with a (male) British agent. He was known as a lady's man in his own community, married to a stunning-looking woman so he was an easy target once his sexual preferences were known.

What was particularly galling back in the day was that it was not uncommon to hear the Dublin government and various unionist politicians publicly state for, obviously, very different reasons, that allegations of security forces colluding with loyalist paramilitaries were nothing more than republican propaganda. These days it is accepted that those claims of collusion were not only factually correct but seriously underplayed.

But as many people have pointed out as well as the political and physical war there was a propaganda war.

Collusion was way more widespread than initially acknowledged and it's naïve, in my opinion, to suggest that the various Dublin governments of whatever political hue, with all their access to various sources of intelligence, were unaware of it in real time.

I would contend that even back then, anyone with half a brain and willing to have a cursory look at what was happening could have seen there was ample evidence to confirm there was a lot more to it than propaganda.

It just didn't suit the narrative of that time.

And the media was part of the big sell of that narrative, that those in uniform were good while those rebelling were bad. If only it were that black and white.

At that time all the main levers of media power were pulled on behalf of the state. The two big broadcasters, BBC and Ulster Television reflected the establishment view, and, as the Troubles broke out, were still largely ignoring the nationalist community. They treated or, at least, tried to treat the North as if it was a homogenous society, often reporting lyrical little pieces about a royal visit or the Balmoral Show and such like, as if it were Devon or Cornwall.

It was outright propaganda, an attempted portrayal of the Six Counties as a pastoral land where peace and harmony reigned. A blind eye was conveniently turned away from the fact royals couldn't visit Derry or Strabane, or that any attempt at a stroll down the Falls Road would have resulted in a riot.

One example of this kind of broadcasting by omission is particularly enlightening of those times. When Down became the first northern team to win the All-Ireland gaelic football title in 1960 and almost 30,000 northerners went down to Dublin for the game the BBC gave the result but had no reporter in Croke Park.

By way of contrast an Irish league soccer match between Crusaders and Coleraine, where it was often three men and a dog in attendance, would have a broadcast from a reporter at the ground to give updates.

In Dublin it was evident that the Conor Cruise O'Brien ethos – he was the minister who introduced Section 31 of the Broadcasting Act which was used to silence Republican voices on RTÉ - seemed to have affected, maybe even infected, the national broadcaster to such an extent that any attempt to portray nationalist or republicans in a sympathetic light was strangled at birth.

It was known a sympathetic attitude could blight some young editor or producer's career, so few were courageous enough to stick their heads above the parapet. President Mary McAleese was to make this very point when, years afterwards, telling of her career in RTÉ.

The story of the IRA's role during the Troubles is well documented so I don't need to reflect on that. But the whole story that led up to the outbreak of the Troubles and the subsequent war on the streets is hugely one-sided and, in my view, dishonest.

As the IRA became more and more effective and the Troubles increased in intensity the tide was very much running against the Republican Movement in particular and the nationalist community in general. The IRA campaign of bombs and shooting was easily explained away as terrorism - and it was – but the context which brought about that campaign was rarely, if ever, explored or explained. Any narrative that might gain sympathy for those engaged in insurrection against the State, against the manifest unfairness and nastiness of the Northern state, was not to be allowed to gain any kind of traction. There had to be a war fought on only one front – against the IRA and the community which supported them.

It came to a head for me when a representative of the Irish News rang me up and asked would we join with them in boycotting IRA death notices. I don't know what sort of pressure he had come under or where it came from but after thinking about it, I said no. I figured how people chose to commemorate their loved ones was a matter for them, not for me.

The overarching memory of it all from those times is that journalistically it was madness, that the abnormal had become the normal.

THE STORY OF JED

I wasn't long at the Journal when it struck me that it was a very serious paper, that there was way too much doom and gloom. It was bit like a Leonard Cohen album which was once described to me as 'music to commit suicide by'.

That a newspaper in an area where a guerrilla war was in full flow might have been a serious publication is a blindingly obvious observation, but one night at home sitting poring over that week's editions I thought the diet of political coverage, reportage of the latest bombings/shooting/ army house raids mixed in with the usual staples of courts, councils etc was so heavy duty as to be almost depressive.

There was no light relief anywhere.

I had the thought that if I was a regular reader of the paper happy pills might be a prerequisite before setting out to peruse each edition. There was enough dark reality for the local community in their daily lives so why buy a paper to read about that dark reality? You heard about a shooting or a bombing? It was the talk of the school, the factory, the workplace – did you really want to buy the Journal to read more about it?

And it also struck me there was no interaction with the local community. The only time an 'ordinary' citizen got a mention was usually when they either got shot or were in court.

The paper was locked in an old-fashioned kind of time warp, not in touch with what was going on in the community. It was all reportage, no interaction. The problem was obvious, the solution much less so.

In the midst of mayhem what's funny? Where's the humour? Could trying to lighten the mood come across as crass and/or insensitive? The Journal reflected that serious side to life in a city where the majority population had long been subjugated by the minority but now things were changing rapidly yet there was little reflection that the nationalist community had largely emerged from that role and that there was a growing confidence out there. We needed just a little something to reflect this.

The solution soon came to me. In fact, it had been staring me in the face all along.

One thing I quickly came to love about the Derry people was that while they were inordinately proud of their city, they also had self-deprecating wit that was as sharp as a tack. I heard witticisms day and daily, usually from within our own staff.

It would frequently run along these lines such as ....

'Q: What do you call a Derry man in a suit? A: The defendant.'

'The first prize in today's Journal's Spot the Ball competition is a week in Derry.. second prize is two weeks.'

One particular day I was out for a walk and a boy and girl, teenagers, just ahead of me were having a slagging match. The girl was clearly the brains of the duo as she absolutely demolished him by saying out loud, well certainly loud enough for me to hear clearly... 'When you were born the doctor should have slapped your mother for bringing such an ugly child into the world.'

It was vicious but brilliantly funny.

It hit me that if I could harness that kind of Derry humour, we could be on to something. It wasn't exactly a eureka moment, but I wrote the very first column at home that night, took it in on the following morning and got it typeset and marked it for page two.

The decision to put it on two was very deliberate. That was where our leader column was and that was usually heavy-duty commentary. I wanted to change this, to reset the dial somewhat by having a tone that reflected light and shade right from the off.

After years of conservatism, I knew the management were unsure about it. I hadn't discussed it with them or with any other staff member. This was a paper that was known to be a serious publication, that was quoted in parliament, was referenced frequently by politicians and academics so it was a concern that this could change the tone, that the gravitas would be diluted if not lost entirely.

With the introduction of JED suddenly there were these little items about teachers coming to class with two different coloured shoes, a cop driving off in the wrong car, the barman who took a sip of a pint of Guinness as he handed it over to a customer. Anything and everything that was off-beat got a mention.

And to my utter amazement it took off like a rocket.

Everyone in Derry had a story they wanted to get in the paper. Colm McCarroll, who had expressed some reservations at the outset, came in one day and remarked that it was becoming a royal pain in the arse, that everywhere he went people were coming up to him and saying, 'here's one for JED'. Despite the pain in the arse, by this stage he had become one of its biggest fans.

And let me put an end to the speculation that went on in Derry for years about JED.

If I had taken a tenner for every time I was asked, was he/she a real person? (was it a pseudonym? was it an acronym for Journal Editorial Department?), I would be a rich man today.

The real story is the first night I wrote it, I didn't want to put my name to it, nor did I want it to be identified who the writer was. It was the sort of column that could easily get you a punch on the nose in a pub or a club if one of its 'victims' learned who had written the story about them.

As I played around with the idea that it was written by the 'Editor of the Derry Journal' the only name that popped out from that combination of words was JED. And as one of the most popular comedy shows of just a few years earlier, the Beverly Hillbillies had a main character called Jed Clampett, I figured it was pretty apt that there would be at least some name recognition factored in.

And there was, right from the off. It struck a chord big time. I was told the first thing everyone went for on getting the paper was the JED Column. And it was considered a considerable coup to be mentioned in it.

Neither did it do any harm that the late Gerry Anderson, who had begun his broadcasting career in Radio Foyle in the early 1980s, made frequent reference in his own inimitable way to items which appeared in the column on his show and that gave it a wider platform.

It got so popular the BBC's main arts and entertainment broadcaster, Sean Rafferty came all the way from Belfast to do a piece where he interviewed me. A photograph later appeared where Rafferty is seen with a microphone interviewing a guy with a paper bag over his head with the word JED written in marker pen.

And even Guildhall Press got in on the act when they decided to publish a book, 'The Best of JED'.

It's obvious now why it was such a success.

Gerry Anderson's show was a massive hit for the exact same reason. In the midst of never-ending reportage of bad news people were hungry for relief, to get away from the relentless barrage of carnage that was the news. Gerry would talk nonsense, interview people who kept hens in the sitting room, talk to bald men as to why they still bought a comb, anything that was light relief. And people loved it, absolutely lapped it up. JED was exactly the same, and it was why it was the first thing most people read when they bought the paper.

Over the years it, unfortunately, was allowed to slip as no one person was assigned the task of writing it and it lost much of its original impact. Too often it was entirely a compilation of little anecdotes submitted by the public with little coordination in terms of either content or style. It was dropped some years after I left and while I understood why that decision was taken, I still regard it as a mistake.

Earlier this year (2023) I was reminded of the enduring appeal of the column when I rejoined the gym at Templemore Sports Complex. I hadn't been there for several years thanks to Covid. On one of the days, I ran into Christine McCamphill who had started out at reception at the complex and we got talking. Straight away she said 'Pat, do you remember that JED item about me?' and of course I did.

I had been standing behind a well-known Derry personality who wanted to book something or other at the facility. At that time, he was regularly on television and in the papers.

Christine, then new to Derry, made the fatal error of innocently asking, 'And who are you?' to which he responded incredulously: 'You mean you don't know who I am?'

I was standing behind him in the queue, and it was like gold dropping out of the sky.

Anyway, one of my favourite JEDs was the story of a Derry City footballer who died and went to Heaven. On arrival at the Pearly Gates, he was asked by St Peter about one of the team's star players.

St Peter: 'What's the difference between God and Eddie Mahon?

Player: 'I don't know. What's the difference between God and Eddie Mahon?'

St Peter: 'God doesn't think he's Eddie Mahon' – I would like to apologise to Eddie for this item!

STORIES FROM 'DOWN UNDER'

The Journal had – and, I hope, still has – an irreplaceable collection of bound newspaper files, some going back to the 1700s. That alone makes it a first source for historians and academics looking to examine life back in the day. Perhaps its biggest claim to fame is that the famous American writer, Leon Uris spent countless hours in the file room researching the background for what was to become his novel *Trinity* which sat atop the New York Times best-selling book charts for about six months in 1976. The book, which was lauded for its historical accuracy, was about the fight for Irish freedom and covered the period 1865 to 1915.

But there is so much more to these files in that there are great human stories hiding under those big bound covers. One night in the file room in the mid-1980s browsing for something else entirely I came across, totally by chance, a picture of a group of about fifty children, all spic and span – hair combed, the boys in suits and ties, girls in lovely dresses with bows in their hair - and the caption said they were from the Nazareth House orphanage in the city and they were being sent to Australia.

This was from the file for 1947.

That picture of those children kind of haunted me for years – what happened to them? Who looked out for them? Why it struck a chord was my eldest was about ten at the time, about the same age as these kids, and the thought of him being sent on his own to Australia got me big time.

About three or four years after coming across this picture the chief reporter, Mary Doherty, walked in and said, 'There's a fella from Australia out here (in the reporters' room) who wants to talk to you for a few minutes.'

For some reason that totally escapes me now I copped on who she was talking about: 'Is that the fucking torture from Melbourne who rang me last year about the bush fires?' I enquired.

Somewhat aghast at the language, Mary replied: 'It's him. For God's sake, keep your voice down. He'll hear you.'

The year before a call had come through from a David Connolly who rang the Journal to say that all the Derry (and Donegal) emigrants living in Australia had survived the worst bushfires in living memory, fires that had caused countless deaths and massive destruction. There was no need for me or anyone in the North West to worry, he had said.

As we didn't circulate in Melbourne, I wasn't aware there was anyone in the Journal worrying in the first place.

Anyway, Connolly - I still think Del Boy from 'Only Fools and Horses' had to be based on him - came in and told me he had a plan to bring home a whole host of Derry/Donegal expats. It was only an idea at that stage, a dream. But he felt that as the years were passing and those who had gone out after the Second World War were now getting to an age where their options of getting home one last time – some, maybe, for the first time even – would be restricted. The vast majority, he explained, who had emigrated from Derry had little education, were in poorly paid blue-collar employment and trips home were beyond the means of all but the few.

'I want the Journal to back me on this,' he explained.

For some reason I agreed and long before the concept became popular, we became his 'media partner' promoting the event. It quickly took on wings.

In 1987 almost 50 people of all ages and from all parts of Australia – some gone for almost a lifetime - came back to Derry on what came to be known as the 'Colmcille Express'. It proved to be a deeply emotional return for many. One girl, an Australian, brought home her son to meet his grandparents for the first time; her husband, their son, had been killed 'Down Under', and the tears rushed like the Foyle as they embraced. I was there that day, and it really was emotional.

Connolly, of course, was absolutely delighted with it all. A long-held ambition had been achieved. And, by this stage, we had become firm friends.

I don't quite recall the circumstances but one day during a conversation I mentioned the picture of the orphaned children. I explained that that picture often came to my mind.

David knew exactly what I was on about, and it certainly struck a chord with him right away as he explained that the treatment of orphans in Australia was now big news back home. Children from these islands had been sent under the euphemistically entitled 'Child Migrant Scheme' to various British colonies but mainly to Australia. The idea of the scheme, which only ended in the late 1960s, was to populate 'the empire' with white stock.

Many months later I got a phone call from him: 'You are not going to believe this McArt…remember our conversation about the child migrants? There's a woman coming to see you, she's one of them – she has a hell of a story to tell.'

And so she had.

In August 1991 I got a call from a receptionist to say that a 'Peggy McFadden, from Melbourne' was in reception. This day turned out to be one of the most unusual days of my life.

In came this little woman who started about 11 a.m. to tell her story and at 2 p.m. I was still listening. That was so unusual – average interview time was about ten minutes then - the Deputy Editor rang in twice wondering if I was okay as I hadn't even taken a comfort break to the toilet.

What had happened was that when Peggy told me she was in that 1947 photo I was totally hooked. I wanted to know what it was all about, what had happened to all those children.

She told a tale of how on the way to Australia the nuns told her that her new name was Peggy not the Margaret she had been christened. They also changed her birthdate and told her that she was an orphan.

She knew she wasn't, so it totally messed with her head.

The whole idea seemed to be to create a false trail so that the children would never be able to retrace their steps in the years to come. They were, by and large, illegitimate and would not be welcome coming back looking for 'respectable' families, finding mothers who had maybe married and moved on with their lives.

Over the years after she left Ireland Peggy told me she hung on to the one thing the nuns couldn't take away - the memory of her older brother, Patrick, who came to the orphanage to take her for a walk every Sunday. Her last memory of him was of a big, red-haired fella of about twelve. She was to spend fifty years looking for him. She haunted emigration records in America and Canada, spent money on private detectives, came home to Ireland in the mid-1980s to search but all to no avail. The trail was dead.

Some years were to pass before she finally got a breakthrough. Because of a change in government policy official documents were made available in Australia.

Armed with the new information that her brother had been fostered out back in the day to a family called Daly in Ballybofey she wrote to the only person she knew with the name Daly, Bishop Edward, asking if he could help her in any way.

Bishop Daly actually rang the parish priest in the Ballybofey area and asked if he had a namesake there only to be told no. He was intrigued by the story and was anxious to help. He told me himself that he then thought what sounded like Ballybofey and, totally on the off chance, decided to ring the parish priest in Ballybay in Co. Monaghan asking the same question. And he struck gold. He got information on Patrick which he then sent by way of a letter to Peggy.

I remember vividly her face and her words as she told me this part of her story: 'The day I got the letter from Ireland I started jumping up and down because I knew they had found him. I tore open the letter and started reading, and then I collapsed. They had found him alright, but he was two years dead at that stage. I think I had a nervous breakdown that day. Fifty years I had spent looking for him, and this is how it ended.'

One horrible coincidence added to the poignancy of the story. Peggy was travelling to Dublin from Derry during her visit to Ireland in the mid-80s and the vehicle she was in developed some mechanical problem. They took the delayed passengers to, of all places, Ballybay while awaiting alternative transport.

It eats away at her to this day: 'I went to a café in that town to get a cup of tea while we waited. I sat looking out the window. Did my brother pass by? Where was he that morning? Imagine I could have gone and hugged and kissed him, something I had wanted to do for fifty years. He was my only living relative on earth.'

You'd have needed a heart of stone not to feel her pain.

Another unforgettable story was that of Jim Breslin, from Perth, who came along a couple of years after Peggy. Jim too was in the 1947 picture but neither he nor Peggy have any recollection of each other on the long journey to the land where, as they were told, 'the sun shone all the time and fruit fell from the trees'.

On the trip out to Australia Jim was accompanied by two of his brothers, the eldest choosing to go of his own accord so that he could look after his two siblings.

When they got to Fremantle in a seeming act of casual cruelty the brothers were separated and sent to different orphanages. It was to be twenty-five years before Jim saw one of them again. He admitted totally that his details of their lives were sketchy in that all he really knew is that one became an alcoholic sleeping rough under the Sydney Harbour Bridge while the other went outback herding sheep living in a tin hut where the temperature in summer could reach almost fifty degrees. So much for keeping siblings together.

A kind, gentle man Jim has been haunted by his early life and the fate that befell his brothers. And his tale of the Christian Brothers stripping naked two children – both aged about seven - who had run away from the orphanage and flogging them in front of the assembled throng is straight out of a Nazi concentration camp nightmare. Jim said the boy next to him shit himself in fright and he was so traumatised by the flogging he became an elective mute for several years, choosing not to speak to anyone.

However, strangest of all the stories was Paddy Dorrian, a feisty wee man from Perth, who was collected by my wife at Belfast airport where, because of his chronic arthritis, he needed a wheelchair.

I had some foreknowledge about his background so thanks to a wee bit of investigation I was able to ascertain that his mother was still alive at that time – this was the mid-1990s – but had not told her family that she had a child before her marriage. There was real drama for about twenty-four hours about what would happen. Thanks to the intervention of a local priest, whom a Journal reporter knew, the path to reconciliation was smoothed after he went to see the mother and explained what was happening.

A meeting was then agreed, to be held away from the prying eyes of neighbours, in neutral territory in Inishowen in Donegal.

The man who had to be ushered off the plane was soon walking up and down the steep hills in Creggan unaided. He, literally, became a changed person; his mother and he had sorted it all out and for the rest of the time he spent in Ireland he spent it with her. He was almost walking on air. Last I heard after he returned to Australia, Paddy went back into the wheelchair.

One final story was that of Mick McGuigan who arrived in my office on a quiet Tuesday afternoon, introduced himself as being one of the child migrants and told me he didn't have a lot of information about his background but had been told I might be able to help. As luck would have it, I could. I told him to give me a couple of hours.

I had got to know a person who, while long retired, had been involved in adoptions in Northern Ireland and was, off the record, able to give me information which pointed me in the right direction.

This particular day after giving details this person was super quick, coming back to me in about 30 minutes, so when Mick came back, I was able to tell him where his family was from. He too found his mother - she was living in England - but it wasn't a successful reunion in that she was clearly hiding something that she was not prepared to share.

The records also revealed that in early childhood Mick was adopted out with another wee fella to a family in the Parish area of Buncrana. I was able to contact the school principal in the area who when Mick and I visited was able to show us his name in Irish on the school roll. The sad thing was that Mick could not remember being at the school or the house where he had lived or even the name of the other wee lad adopted with him. For whatever reason it had all been wiped from his memory.

Sitting in David's house in Melbourne in 1989 with a few guests drinking a couple of cans of 'Swan's Melbourne Bitter' he started telling his friends these stories.

And he told of our first meeting, casually stating: 'And do you realise he called me that 'fucking torture from Australia'?'

All these years he had known that but had never mentioned it.

'How did you know?' I queried, more than a little bit embarrassed.

David was profoundly deaf and had two large hearing aids. They were primitive but back then one side effect was that they enabled him to pick up random sounds from around a room, as if someone was using a microphone only he could hear.

I hadn't known that.

McArt liked to get some exercise in at lunchtime to clear his head - heading out for a run, swim or, in later years, a big walk. Oftentimes his post-lunchtime appointments - in this case Martin McGuinness - had to wait while he took a shower.

Jim Guy, the independent unionist mayor of Derry, on a courtesy visit to the Journal offices in 1987 with his wife Doreen. Included are Frank Curran, Colm McCarroll, Pat McArt, Frank McCarroll and Aileen McManus. Guy had been expelled from the Ulster Unionist Party for refusing to boycott the renamed 'Derry' City Council.

Editors at large: in the inner sanctum with visiting former Irish Press chief Tim Pat Coogan and his own predecessor in the Journal chair, Frank Curran.

Sinn Féin president Gerry Adams and the Assembly Member for Foyle (later Stormont Speaker) Mitchel McLaughlin meet McArt and Jounal director Jean Long on a visit to the Journal in 2005.

With Colm McCarroll on a visit to inspect an Eastern European factory ship berthed on Lough Swilly in 1982. There were claims that the facility was staffed by prisoners, or by workers who had been offered the job as an alternative to prison.

The veteran Journal photographer Larry Doherty captures an impromptu Irish Dancing session in the newsroom, after the 1984 Christmas edition had been sent to print. Among the audience are Peter Doran, Pat McArt, Frank Curran and Siobhan McEleney (partially hidden). Despite the relaxed atmosphere, no alcohol is ever allowed on the Journal premises (officially...)

Thumbs up for the photographer during the first Journal Two Bridges Run in 1984.

McArt found Martin McGuinness a brave and principled person, and the two would become trusted friends - despite the fact that the Journal man's politics would in many respects have been closer to John Hume's.

Fundraising heroes: in 1990, McArt along with Tom McGInley, his son Ciaran McGinley and Bernie Mount all ran the London Marathon to raise money for Derry's fledgling Foyle Hospice. They collected more than £21,000, which at that time was the biggest single donation to the hospice. Shortly after, Tom McGinley was named Donegal Person of the Year.

Taking part in BBC Radio Ulster's Talkback programme with presenter David Dunseith, Glenn Barr, Declan O'Hare and Jimmy Cadden, Editor of the Londonderry Sentinel.

With the runner and internationally-renowned mediator Brendan Duddy, watching Derry athlete Bobby Farren's attempt to run a four-minute mile at the Templemore Sports Complex in 1995. (He missed out narrowly.) The BBC's Peter Taylor would later make the programme The Secret Peacemaker about Duddy's work as the clandestine contact between the IRA and the British government.

From a land Down Under: Derry expats, George & Colleen Hudson (originally from Claudy and Tullyally) and their son Daren and his wife Kylie, on a visit to the Journal offices in the 1990s. McArt had first met the couple during his trip to Australia in 1989, and they have been friends since.

Pat and Rosie McArt presenting visitor Jeremy Corbyn with a Donegal tweed scarf, when he visited their home in Burt in 2022.

The Northern Ireland Secretary, Dr Brian Mawhinney, chats with Deputy Editor Mary McLaughlin, on a visit to the Journal in 1992. McArt got on well with the Conservative minister, who had grown up in Belfast. A nuclear physicist, Mawhinney later became a peer and was chair of the Football League.

Recruiting Derry GP and Foyle Hospice founder Tom McGinley as medical director of the 1985 Journal Foyle Five [mile-race]. The two men regularly went running together at lunchtime, along with Brendan Duddy.

At the computer is Paddy Dorian, who was shipped to Australia from Derry as a child migrant in the 1940s. McArt's work in highlighting the scandal of the forced migrations had led to many expats returning to Ireland to retrace their roots. Included in the picture are John McManus, of the Journal Advertising Department, and Joe Martin, Production Manager. Paddy Dorian arrived back in Derry in a wheelchair but was so buoyed up by reconnecting with his mother, who had been told he had died, he was walking up and down Creggan Hill before he left.

Making a presentation to Willie O'Connell, on his retirement in 1993. O'Connell served as Mayor of Derry (1982-83) while working with the Journal.

Three Patricks and a Bertie. Father, son and grandson McArt meet with Taoiseach Ahern at an event in Letterkenny in the 1990s.

Hard at work as the irreverent columnist Jed, who brought many a smile to Derry faces during the dark days - and the occasional lawsuit to the DJ...

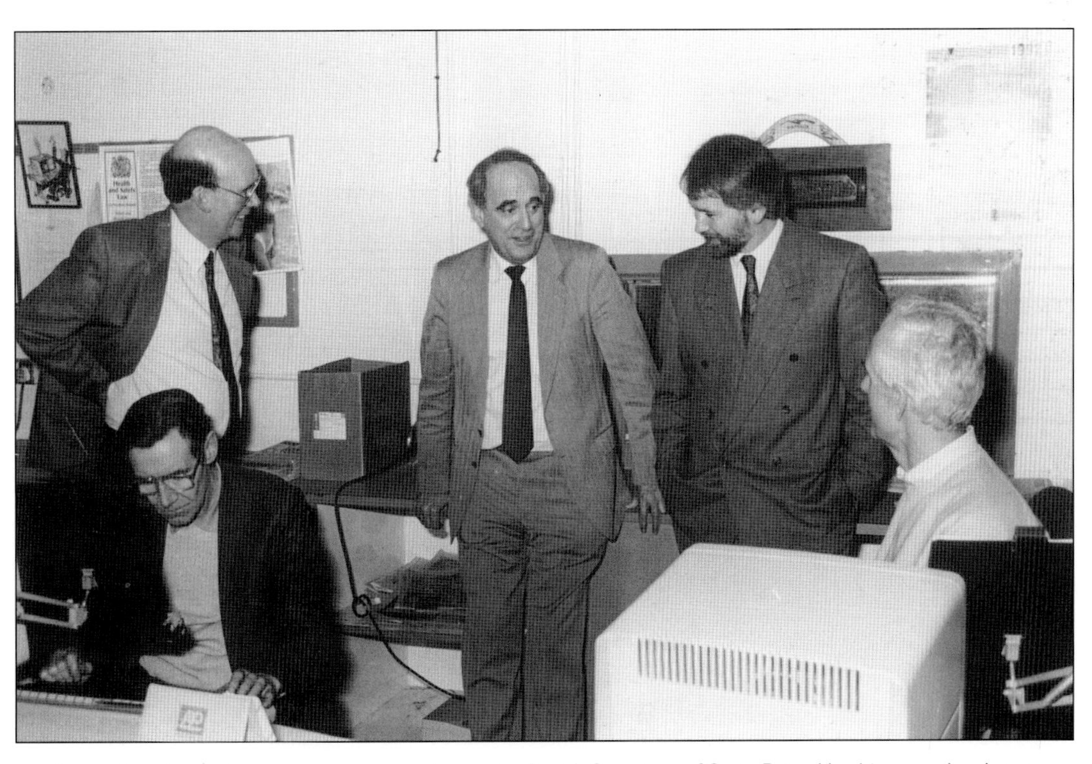

Compositor Jimmy Conway pays no attention to the British Secretary of State Brian Mawhinney as he chats to Gerry Gallagher during his visit to the Journal in 1992.

The American lobby visited Derry regularly throughout the 1990s - and would even call into McArt's book launches. On this occasion Congressman Joe Kennedy II is enjoying the launch of McArt's Irish Almanac of Facts.

Saying goodbye to reporter Mark McFadden on his last day at the Journal before heading off to UTV. McFadden famously had to learn to drive in about a week to qualify for the new post.

Colm McCarroll, who would become Journal MD and later establish the Derry News, realised the importance of his editor having a public profile. After McArt's appointment, he would encourage his protégé to become the face of the Journal, such as during this investigative visit to an Eastern European factory ship, off Rathmullan, in 1982.

With fellow writers, Darach MacDonald, Eamonn McCann and Emmett McCourt at a book launch at Ráth Mór in Creggan in 2015 (Photo by Phil Cunningham).

Signing a copy of the Irish Almanac and Yearbook of Facts for Martin McGuinness. McArt co-edited the book in 1997 and 1998 with Donal Campbell

John Hume was a regular visitor to the Journal offices and often brought high-profiled visitors from all over the world along with him. In this case, his companions are the Taoiseach Garret FitzGerald and the Foreign Minister Peter Barry.

BBC Northern Ireland's Sean Rafferty (now Radio 3) interviews 'JED' about his notorious satirical column. Despite the disguise, JED's big Donegal hands end up giving the game away...

In May 2023, McArt was accorded a civic reception and presented with a special award by Sandra Duffy, Mayor of Derry & Strabane, in recognition of his contribution to the North West media sector.

Journal MD Frank McCarroll presenting Creggan man - and celebrated international runner - Paul Craig with his prize for winning the inaugural Journal Foyle Five in 1983. McArt was himself a useful long-distance runner and recorded a time of under 34 minutes in the race, which prompted 'Old Man' McCarroll to present him with a silver tankard as a memento.

What the hell just happened...? Photographer Paddy Stevenson captures a slightly-dazed McArt off-guard.

Newell McBride receives the 1984 Derry Journal Golf Society trophy from MD Frank McCarroll. Watching on enviously are Colm McCarroll, Pat McArt, Brian McCarroll (both McCarroll brothers were talented amateur golfers and could have gone professional if allowed), John Gill, Eamon Davis, Gerry Gallagher, Cecil McGill, Arthur Duffy and John McManus.

In January 2022, while in Derry to speak at the Bloody Sunday 50th Anniversary commemorations, the former Labour leader Jeremy Corbyn visited McArt's home in Donegal to take part in the former Journal boss's weekly podcast with Jude Collins. Clockwise are Jeremy Corbyn, Alison Stoecker (Labour special advisor), Pat McArt, Barry James of the Peace & Justice Project, and Mr Corbyn's wife Laura Alvarez.

Presenting the Buncrana Hearts Ladies Team with their Journal-sponsored five-a-side trophy in 1983.

With his friend, the Journal's Australian correspondent and migrant champion David Connolly, at the legendary Ettamogah Pub, in Albury, New South Wales.

Pat and Rosie at Journal staffer Pauline Higgins' wedding, just after the new editor had taken up the hot seat.

In 1985, the Journal was at the forefront of Derry's efforts to raise funds for famine-hit Ethiopia. McArt is meeting here with members of the international relief charity Concern, including local doctor Raymond McClean and Fr Jack Finucane.

Clann Mhic Airt at the Sydney Harbour Bridge in 1999.

Ann McLaughlin (Derry Journal administrator), Pat and Rosie McArt, and Joe McLaughlin (Director of Northside Developments) meeting up among the huge crowds on Guildhall Square the day Bill Cllinton first came to Derry in November 1995

Men of renown: Garret the Good, Saint John and Blessed Pat on a walkabout in Derry in 1985.

New technology allowed reporters to design pages on their own computers. The automation of production processes, along with the introduction of colour printing, was one of many changes in the Journal landscape during the 1990s.

HERE'S 50 PENCE SON!

I suppose I should have known emigration – and Australia in particular – were to play a major part in my life when in 1974 my first major interview, as I would have described it back then, was a lovely story.

Up until then as a cub reporter I was confined to, in the main, typing out sports reports so it was a real step up when I was sent to get the story of a woman from Letterkenny who, at the age of 74, was taking her first trip on an aeroplane. And what a first trip – all the way to Australia!

Mrs Duggan had three of her sons emigrate there in the years soon after the Second World War. She was a lovely woman and it turned out to be a great interview. She admitted to being nervous going on the 'big plane' but the joy on her face at the prospect of seeing her children again would have been evident to a blind person.

I even got a story from her when she came back when she told me she had a great time in Australia and what a lovely place it was. She even insisted as I left on giving me 50p, to get myself a cup of tea. She had loved the story I had done about her trip.

It had gone down a storm and I got plenty of comment about the 'lovely story'.

Years passed and then one day out of the blue I met another of Mrs Duggan's children, Colm, still living in Donegal. I recounted my tale of having interviewed his mother twice. He looked at me oddly before remarking, 'You know, she never told you the truth...the real story.'

I asked him what he was on about, that to me she had seemed delighted with her excursion Down Under.

He retorted that he had the real story: 'When my mother landed in Sydney, she had to take another flight to Queensland. When she landed there, she waited and waited for my eldest brother to come collect her. Time passed and then there were only a couple of people left in the small passenger reception area when she noticed a man standing still searching for someone. That person was her son, my brother. The years had changed them so much they didn't recognise each other.

'She was looking to see the dark-haired young fella and he was now grey haired while he was looking for the mother of his childhood and didn't recognise the old woman standing there.'

He told me his mother cried for years about it.

This is a story I have always remembered in that it taught me one great lesson: not everything – or everyone – is what it might first appear.

TRAGEDY COMES TO MY DOOR

Being the Editor of a newspaper in a place where violent death is far from uncommon breeds a kind of defence mechanism in that for your own mental stability you learn not to get too emotionally caught up, to develop a distance from tragedy – well, at least you try to. It's the only way to survive.

But that distancing doesn't always work, and when death comes to your own door the kind of mental gymnastics needed are totally useless. Your defences are totally shot down. And suddenly, you get a front row seat of what real tragedy means.

Josephine Porter (née McLaughlin) could be a bit of a torture on occasion. On Saturday mornings while I was trying to have a quiet lie-in after a week of head spinning chaos there was usually a noise explosion about 10am. I didn't need to be told what it was, or who it was. Josephine, my wife's sister, had arrived.

She would enter our house like a dervish, full of energy and noise. The peace and tranquillity of a Saturday morning lie-in was gone. I often thought left alone with her for five minutes and no witnesses, God knows what I would have done.

That was her public persona. It took me years to realise I didn't know the real Josephine at all.

I attended Josephine's wedding with my then girlfriend, Rosie, and while I don't remember the day that well, one thing I do recall is that it was a source of some amusement to quite a few of the guests that Josephine, small, dark and pretty, was marrying a toy boy, George Porter. He was only a teenager then; she was in her twenties.

After they got married, they moved firstly back to Dublin and then to Leicester where George worked with Josephine's brother, Jimmy, who had a contracting business.

By the time they returned to Ireland about six years later, they had two children, and nothing would do Josephine other than to build a house on a site close to George's family home outside Buncrana. She wanted a nest, a place her family could grow up in.

It was a project she put her heart and soul into. I wasn't an interested party in this construction, but I overheard non-stop discussions between herself and Rosie about the cost of materials, colour of curtains, how much carpet would be needed etc. There wasn't a builder's yard in the county she didn't know. But it turned out to be worth it when after years of scrimping and saving she eventually achieved her ambition – a new house. Everything, it seemed, was on the rise.

Things got even better when within weeks of moving into her new residence she learned she was pregnant with her third child. Now, she really was on a roll. So, it seemed only a routine, run-of-the-mill thing when she became unwell a couple of months into the pregnancy, eventually having to be hospitalised.

On the following Sunday, a couple of days after she had been admitted to Letterkenny General Hospital, as I was lazing around the house the phone rang.

It was Josephine who didn't really seem herself, none of the usual banter: 'Pat, is Rosemary there?'

I replied: 'She's on her way up to see you with (her sisters) Mary and Teish.'

Detecting something in her voice I asked, rather stupidly and casually, because I was still watching ITV's big soccer show - this was mid 1980s - out of the corner of my eye: 'Is there something wrong?'

With a voice shaking she replied hesitantly: 'Yeah, I think there is .....the consultant wants to speak urgently to me and George.....and that's not good, is it? He says he's coming back ...to see us tonight.' It was the staccato speech pattern that got me fully focused. That was not Josephine in any shape or form.

Hospital consultant coming in on a Sunday night - that wasn't normal, was it? Even I knew that was highly unusual. Now, I no longer was distracted and was tuned-in, I could hear only too clearly the apprehension in her voice. I really don't remember much more of the conversation, but I probably muttered some meaningless platitudes about being sure everything would be alright and not to worry. I was confident it would be as I had no other experience to go on, to compare it to.

Little did I know that this was the start of a long journey where there was a destination but not a happy ending. I recall the hours passing slowly and the bad vibes began to gather when instead of being home by four a clock as originally stated – visiting was supposed to be only for an hour in the afternoon back then – Rosie and her sisters still had not returned by late in the evening.

Finally, near midnight they arrived back to our house in Culmore, just outside Derry city, pale and drawn, anxiety clearly written on their faces. Highly unusual too was the near silence as they filed through the front door into the hallway.

I remember this as clearly as a scene from a film where the action comes to a complete halt: 'Josephine has leukaemia,' Rosie said finally.

All I can say now is that this was a massive life-changing, even life-defining moment for our family. Everything changed after that.

Up until this I had lived in some cloud-cuckoo land in regard to the vagaries of human health. Surely, young people like us didn't get cancer? That only happened to old people, like my Grandad. It sounds so ridiculous, but this was the first time I had to confront, on an internal level, the fact that cancer could get anyone – young or old. It didn't discriminate. That realisation actually frightened me.

And, within hours, for the first time in my life also I was to learn first-hand of real human courage.

I was at work the following day when a friend who worked at the hospital rang to tell me that that morning as she was leaving for Dublin for specialist treatment, Josephine, almost literally, danced out of the ward chatting and waving to patients and nurses she had got to know. Despite her own fears she was, my friend said, putting on a show for everyone

Josephine put up a great battle for almost two years but eventually the leukaemia claimed her. She was only thirty-three. The pregnancy which had first taken her to the doctors had tragic results too in that the child died and she was so ill she could not even attend the funeral.

Originally, for a few weeks, there had been good news, a remission in the cancer. We all took hope from that. Josephine even came home, and life went back to a kind of normal. Ever anxious to help others, she did an interview for a local programme about her experiences, and she went fundraising for the hospital to various events.

But it wasn't to last. A couple of months into remission she became unwell, and a blood test revealed the bad news. The leukaemia was back. And she had to go back to Dublin. She never came home again.

On the day she was leaving to return to St Vincent's Josephine took her two children, Desmond and Damien to our house in Derry. The day was a cold grey day in early Spring, and I came home for lunch. Shortly after Josephine and George and the boys, who were only about ten and eight at the time, arrived we sat down to eat but no one was very hungry, and there was a sort of forced gaiety. I suppose, in our individual ways, we were all trying to ignore the large elephant in the room.

Eventually it came time to go and as she was leaving Rosie, very movingly, said: 'Josephine, don't worry about the boys. I'll look after them for you.'

Josephine turned back and looking Rosie straight in the face, said very deliberately and very clearly: 'Rosemary, I know that as long as they are with you, they'll be alright.'

With that she got into the car and George drove away. I don't think she even looked back. She probably couldn't.

Rosie and I only saw Josephine once more after that.

We took the children up to see her in Dublin some months later, but she was so ill that day I'm still not sure she was aware they, or we, were there. I remembered she smiled when she saw us but that was about it.

I never said it to Rosie, but I knew then – and I'm sure Rosie did too – that Josephine was not going to make it. Allied to a horrible illness the chemotherapy and the radium treatment had devastated her physically. She was emaciated, tubes everywhere, her hair long gone. But like every human in such a situation we kept hoping for a miracle. The old adage 'where there is life there is hope' was very much to the fore. But it was to be in vain.

One Friday night, only a couple of weeks after she had gone back to St Vincent's, and with Rosie only weeks away from full-term pregnancy, the phone rang out in the hall, and I went to answer it. It was Gerry, Rosie's brother, ringing from England in an agitated state asking could I confirm if Josephine had died; he had been told that by someone who knew the family in Dublin and who had contacted him.

Rosie came out, mimed 'who is that?' and I had to tell her he had been told Josephine had passed on. To this day I recall her profound anguish.

Three days later we buried Josephine in the cemetery outside Buncrana that is known as 'The Parish'. She's buried with her son.

In the days that followed it was said that the only time she ever got to use the front door of her new house was the day she came out of it in her coffin.

In the years that followed her two boys stayed a lot with us. Our two boys, Shane and Aaron, almost matched perfectly in age Desmond and Damien, and they were all firm friends. Neither of us ever forgot Josephine's last words. It was a bond neither of us would ever, nor even wanted, to break to her.

Little over a week after Josephine's death Rosie gave birth to Paddy, our third son. Her labour began early on Good Friday 1988, and it turned out to be a long delivery running into about five am the following day. Paddy's arrival was a welcome distraction for us all. It was a very, very tough time for Rosie but having our own two, and Desmond and Damien plus the new baby meant that she had to put her sorrow aside and get on with looking after everyone. I honestly cannot imagine the pain she was in emotionally, but I witnessed then that my wife was a much deeper, tougher, more caring person than even I had thought.

Over those following years maybe on a Friday night when we were sitting having a glass of wine to mark the end of the working week Rosie would, for some inexplicable reason, launch into one of her theories: 'Josephine's story is not finished. There's something not right here, Pat. Something's not right.'

I would try to explain it away as wishful thinking. Or the wine was playing with her mind. 'No,' would come the response with the same logic every time, 'our Josephine was a planner. She knew she was dying. Why did she not write us a letter? Why did she not write a will? Why didn't she ring us up? There's something that doesn't add up. Something is not right. There's something else there.'

I should have known better than to doubt her instincts.

Well over a decade was to pass when I got a call out of the blue from George Porter, Josephine's husband. This was on a Thursday evening at work and, as usual, I didn't have a lot of time for chitchat. He got straight to the point.

'McArt, what are you doing tomorrow? Fancy a pint?'

It was such an unusual request I said I would be delighted.

By this stage George had remarried and had another child. We had been in touch on occasions, but we had largely gone our separate ways. But I knew there was something going on, so I was really intrigued.

When George called at our home for me on the Friday, he ran into both Rosie and another of Josephine's sisters, Anna. They had a cup of tea while waiting for me to get back from the Journal. On my arrival we soon left for the '19th Hole', at Bridgend - there are a couple of golf courses not too far away, hence the pub's name – where we settled in a little booth. We chatted about politics, the weather, just about anything under the sun and when, on my third pint (I remember that very clearly) I was sober enough to get out the statement: 'By the way, George, what did you want to see me about? Another pint and you won't get a sensible response from me.'

It was then I noticed that his hands were shaking as he reached into an inside pocket of his jacket and pulled out an envelope from which he removed a photo. 'Have a look at that....', says he. I picked up the picture and, totally stupid, remarked: 'That's Josephine...'

He suggested 'look again' – and then it was all too clear that it wasn't Josephine.

The girl in the photo had obviously just graduated from university as she was pictured with a mortar board and cloak. It was obvious too that it was highly unlikely to be Ireland seeing it was in brilliant sunshine. More than a little confused at the remarkable resemblance between this girl and Josephine, I then asked: 'If that's not Josephine, who is she?'

'That', said George, 'is our daughter.'

'Jesus, you've got to be joking…'

The shock had totally neutralised the alcohol by now and the questions kept pouring out. When had this happened? How had it happened? Where had it happened?

Out it came. The short version was that he was 18 and Josephine 21 when they discovered she was pregnant. Back then pregnancy outside marriage was taboo, a real source of scandal. It was the era of Magdalene laundries, back-street abortions in England or emigration to a far-off place. They had set off for Dublin telling both sets of parents that they were looking for work as neither, quite truthfully, could get gainful employment locally.

After whatever discussions they had, it was agreed that the best was to give up the child for adoption. It was a decision Josephine was to come to bitterly regret.

So, what had happened? George told me his story.

George: 'When Josephine was dying, she made me promise I would go look for our daughter. We used to talk about it a lot over the years. Josephine knew that once a child was eighteen, they could legally look for their parents and vice versa and if it was agreeable to both parties a meeting could be arranged.'

So why had he left it so long?

'I got scared. I thought let sleeping dogs lie, that I might be doing more harm than good now. If she is with a good family, me coming in now might destroy something. I kept putting it off.'

So, what changed his mind?

'Josephine. I couldn't sleep at night. I would keep having this dream where she was telling me, 'You promised me……'

George said his head got so fried he eventually went to an old nun he knew who lived in a convent near his home and told her the story. On its completion she told him it was only too obvious what he should do, wasn't the mother of his child telling him as clear as day: 'Go find our daughter.'

Some months earlier George had made initial attempts to get the search up and running but it had been slow going. He felt one social worker in the adoption service had been less than helpful making some kind of moral judgement about having a child out of wedlock or whatever. It was God's punishment for sinners that the child had to be given up for adoption. Eventually, she was moved on and a young lady from the North took over his case. He found her much more empathetic.

Still unsure of where he was at in this particular journey the last thing George had expected was that one day he would find a letter on his hall floor from the adoption service telling him that they had located his daughter.

'What do I do now?' was paramount.

He was told that they had written to his daughter, who was living abroad, informing her that someone was looking for her and was she interested in taking it any further? The adopted person has, quite rightly, the right to refuse to meet the person seeking them out and has the right to insist that their identity is not revealed. George's and Josephine's biological daughter obviously wanted to know about her past. She wanted to take it to the next stage.

So, what now? Why was he telling me?

George: 'I have to write her a letter telling her about me and Josephine. And that's where you come in. I want you to write it for me.'

Before I answered that I was only too aware that there was something massive we needed to do.

'George, we have to tell Rosie There is no way I'm keeping this a secret.'

I knew that if I made any attempt to hide this it would, possibly, kill our marriage. This was the woman who had, in reality, become Desmond and Damien's mother, who had fought for them, loved them, fed them, even clothed them when she thought it necessary; she was doing it all in the name of her dead sister. I was not going to mess with that. If I attempted to hide this and anything went wrong, how would I ever explain I knew and didn't tell her?

We left the pub immediately and made our way to my home where I was seriously disturbed to learn that Anna, who had been there earlier, had left. I had hoped she would be there so that Rosie and she could have been a support for each other.

When we came in the door Rosie was watching something or other on the television.

'Do you two want something to eat?' she asked as she stood near the cooker ready to put on our usual Friday evening meal.

'We have something to tell you, Rosie,' says I, adding quickly 'it's nothing bad.'

It was a moronic thing to say, but I was totally flustered. I was trying to get across that it was both bad news and good news involved here almost simultaneously, but I was totally aware this was not a 'you've won the lotto' moment either.

Suddenly there was a definite anxiety in the room

I told George: 'Show her the photograph....'

I think something dawned right away on a deep level with Rosie despite the confusion and tension in her mind.

'Who is this?' she asked as she looked at the picture.

'That's Josephine...and George's ...daughter...,' I replied.

'It can't be? how can it be?' she responded. And then as the realisation of what she was seeing hit home she burst into tears.

So, Rosie's intuition was right all along; she did know her sister better than any of us.

Over the next 24 hours Rosie told the story to her family. It turned out one member of the family had known the story but had given Josephine his word never to reveal it and, very honourably, had kept it even though it must have cost him emotionally, particularly at the time she was dying.

A couple of days later I got a call from George again. He wanted to get the letter off and see what would happen. It was a far-from-simple request. What do you tell someone about a mother they have never met? A mother who gave them up for adoption? Are they going to believe a word you say? And if there is no response, can someone blame you? That you pitched it all wrong.... you should have said this, you shouldn't have said that.

In due course the letter was dispatched to an address far from Ireland. It was responded to quickly and despite some initial fears, very positively. It was eventually agreed that there would be a reunion of sorts, that they would meet.

On a beautiful warm summer's day months later D Day arrived. I don't know how George and Rosie felt but driving that day to a hotel in Letterkenny where the meeting was to take place my heart was pounding so fast I, genuinely, had a feeling that I was having a coronary.

But in the midst of all the emotion and the knowledge that this was human tragedy on a grand scale, the journalist in me was also thinking this story had everything - a long lost daughter, a dead mother, a father meeting a daughter for the first time in more than 20 years, two brothers meeting a sister for the first time. Hollywood couldn't have written this one.

Unlike Hollywood this, unfortunately, is real life. Like all these stories there is no single, happy ending that everyone would like. Lives lived differently make different people of us all. It went well but George's daughter was their biological daughter, not their 'real' daughter. Her parents were the people who loved her, who raised her, who comforted her at night, who paid for her education, who did the right thing by her. And they did it very well. She was, is, a lovely girl. But as the old Jesuit saying goes, 'Give us the child and we'll give you the man'.

So it proved here.

Their daughter had a very different life from that of her two siblings, had lived in various countries and had the comfort blanket of a secure and loving family unaware of the tragedy of her biological family.

One final postscript, around 2005 Josephine's son, Damien, got married in Scotland. It was lovely that his only sister, her husband, and her children plus her parents came too. It was all captured wonderfully on video.

Our son Shane was best man. His speech that day was one of the funniest I had ever heard at a wedding, he having the place in stitches when he did a laptop presentation of some key months in Damien's life complete with commentary that did not miss the intended target even once. It was hilarious.

Indeed, it was all going swimmingly until he came to the part he couldn't avoid, Josephine. He started by saying something like 'I can't let a day like this pass without pointing out the one person who is missing.... Josephine'.

Shane and Damien are best friends, and I knew how often they must have talked about Josephine and how deep Damien's hurt about not having his mother there that day – indeed for most of his life - was. He told how he and Damien had become like brothers, how they spent a lot of time together and how much Damien missed his mother.

Tears started to run down Shane's cheek and as I looked around, I saw almost everyone else was crying too. Strange as it may seem it was cathartic, the beginning of healing. A lot of things that needed to be said got said that day. Damien said he wanted to say publicly that he loved Rosie, that she had become a mother to him – he still sends her a card on Mother's Day -- and that he wanted people to know that.

The cynics can say what they like but I felt Josephine was there in spirit that day. You could almost feel her presence.

The love in that room for her was palpable and if she had been hanging around waiting for it all to be sorted, I would think she crossed over to the other side that day.

It was closure.

YOU COULDN'T MAKE IT UP

I was only in the door one morning when the phone rang. On the line was an RUC Inspector who worked in the Press Office in Derry wanting to know if we had a young reporter, let's call him Danny Boyle (definitely not his real name) working for us. I said yes, and then asked the usual question: 'Why do you want to know?'

'My boss has just been on,' says the RUC man, 'and he told me to tell you that we are thinking of charging your lad with being an *agent provocateur*.'

I thought I had heard every possible complaint about behaviour of reporters up until then, but this was definitely one coming in totally out of left field.

Turns out the night before Danny had gone to a stand-off between nationalist protestors and loyalists in the Waterside area of Derry. This was during the marching season, and he had, apparently, strolled between the warring factions whispering incendiary comments about 'the other side' as he went along – he told the loyalists what the Fenians were doing, and vice versa. As the police had plain-clothed officers in the crowd who had heard both versions of his conversations, they sure weren't happy.

While officially a reporter, I was told he also had a camera with him – which was in total contravention of NUJ rules in what was then a very unionised industry – so he was obviously also looking for a few good shots when the action sparked off.

That was a great start to a morning. But it was to get progressively worse.

Later the same day a woman rang. Again, the question – 'Have you a reporter called Danny Boyle?'

'Yip.'

'Well,' she said 'he was up here the other night, and he told some people he was doing a story about the dangers of bonfires, and he tried to get some children to jump over the flames. One of them was mine.'

By this stage I was asking myself – is this guy for real?

This lady was not amused at all. And she was letting me know that if anything had happened to her child it would not be a conversation she would be having with me as Editor or with Danny but something much more serious.

When a solicitor rang about an hour later threatening to sue on behalf of a client, I knew a bad day was just about to get worse. Turns out in this case

Danny had reported that a group of Dublin soccer fans up for a game against Derry City had provocatively put a tricolour out a window in a mainly loyalist area of the Waterside. The only part of the story that was true and accurate was that they were fans of a Dublin soccer club

What had happened was the lads had gone to the Waterside, had booked into a B&B, had a tricolour which they carried everywhere placed on the windowsill, not hanging out the window. They had placed it there like they would have done with a shirt or a pair of trousers. There was no deliberate provocation, no flying the flag out the window to stir up trouble. But it could be seen from the street, and our lad had seen it going through the area and decided to do a bit of fictional reporting.

The owner of the B&B had, following the report, received threats from loyalists, had to close her business over a busy weekend and was intending to sue for compensation for losses incurred.

The next day I had to suggest to Danny he look for another job. Three complaints in a year about any journalist would have been pretty heavy duty but three in a day?

Oddly enough he was a decent enough skin about getting the sack, suggesting himself that maybe this journalism lark wasn't for him.

I couldn't have agreed more.

Last I heard he's living in Australia or New Zealand, somewhere which is just about far enough away. Hopefully, he's washing dishes or keeping chickens, something where he can't get near a computer.

On the other side there were people who could make your day. One of these was Paddy Stevenson, a very talented artist whose day job was working as a Journal photographer. Taking photos of Pioneer Pin awardees or Feis winners could be banal in the extreme but to lighten the boredom load Paddy used to try and come at things from a different angle. And that, for me, made him a great newspaper man. He could also be very, very funny.

Liam Gallagher had to be just about the most idiosyncratic journalist that ever lived. From my first day back in June 1974 Liam was a constant companion in my daily life until his premature death not too many years later. He had been the archetypal brightest boy in the town winning a scholarship to secondary school and then on to university to study medicine. He was doing brilliantly in Med school until he and several others were involved in a road smash on the way home from a dance and that was a brilliant medical career over.

As he said himself, he lost the ability to concentrate for long, sustained periods which was an absolute requirement for the study of medicine. Journalism, by way of contrast, suited him like a glove.

He used to go to court but rarely had a notebook. As I said in an earlier chapter, most cases were recorded on backs of old, used Major cigarette packets.

I suppose it is a cliché but these days most reporters have laptops, mobile phones, use Facebook and Twitter and email and while that's the way of the world now I would contend most, if not all, the individuality has gone. The over-application of political correctness has had a Stepford Wives effect on journalism; everyone is orthodox; no rocking the boat in case it affects the career.

I would, and could, cogently argue the case that the people I knew years ago were much more interesting, had more character, than most of the college educated graduates who pass for journalists these days. It is only my opinion but I stand by it.

FOR SUCCESS, GET SMART

The old joke about the Italian army chief in WW2 who kept a bullet in the chamber of his gun to shoot his second-in-command always struck me as comical. He was ensuring no upstart was going to replace him in the top job. It might have been funny, but it wasn't very smart. I believed in the exact opposite. Surround yourself with smart people if you want to succeed.

And I had plenty of smart people to choose from.

Two people who stand out in this regard were, as I referred to at the start of this book, Siobhan Quinn and Domhnall MacDermott. They were both as bright as you could possibly wish for, both in touch with what was happening on the ground and though I didn't know it at the time, both fiercely competitive.

Siobhan was from the heart of the Bogside, and from a working-class background. She did well at school and was part of that first generation of working families who got the opportunity to go to university.

Domhnall was the son of one of one of the best-known doctors in Derry, a member of a house which produced lawyers and journalists like a production line. He was an unbelievable character – funny, often narky, often kind, and surprisingly wise.

They were friends long before they came to work at the Journal. Much of that friendship was cemented in their teenage years over drinks in the Dungloe Bar.

Both came from Republican families and, because of that, could get inside information like no one else could. Thanks to them, I could tell what way the political wind was blowing long before anyone heard the weather forecast.

The story of how they came to work at the paper shows an almost symbiotic relationship that endured their entire lives. They were joined at the hip in so many strange ways.

Advertisements for reporters were relatively rare at the Journal but when one did appear we were usually inundated with responses. In 1980 one such advertisement was published and amongst the huge numbers responding were Domhnall and Siobhan.

As they both had university degrees and were local, they were called for interview.

Domhnall, I was told, got a letter on a Friday morning informing him he had been successful and was being offered a position. Feeling delighted he was also somewhat abashed at the prospect of telling his best friend that as there was only one position available, she had not got the job.

Off he strolls around to Quigg's Florist shop on William Street where Siobhan had a summer job to tell her the news and when he walks in, he says something along the lines that he was bringing both good news and bad news.

'What's the good news?' asked his old pal.

'I got the job with the Journal,' he replied.

With that Siobhan whips out a letter from her pocket: 'And so did I.'

Colm McCarroll had been so impressed with them both that he decided to employ both. It was to prove a great decision. Once in employment they delivered big time.

I only learned much later how competitive they were. At the end of each year, they totted up who had the most lead stories and whoever topped the list got a free night out at the other's expense. That must have happened for the best part of a decade.

It was a total shock when we learned Domhnall, who hadn't been keeping well, had cancer. Life had been on the up for him. He had settled down and had only been married to Sheila a very short time, when the diagnosis was made. At the start there were a lot of optimistic noises about recovery, but it wasn't to be. When he passed, we were all devastated. He was a huge character, a one-off type.

Siobhan was the opposite of Domhnall. She was as sensible as a rock. She was also as trustworthy and loyal as you could find on this earth. When the long-serving Mary McLaughlin resigned as Deputy Editor to concentrate on her growing family Siobhan was appointed to the role and she was to prove an absolute godsend.

She had tremendous ability, got on brilliantly with both the public and the staff, knew how to head trouble off at the pass and was able to keep me on the straight and narrow. No mean feat, all things considered.

She also had an uncanny ability to sniff out trouble. Some days she would come into my office and warn me to watch my back, that someone was stirring up strife either in the reporters' office or out on the floor. I needed to get it sorted straight away.

She would also tell me if I had been unfair to someone, that I needed to call them in and explain why I had done what I had done. She was kindness personified, but not that soft. If someone who was messing about needed sorted, she could do that too. Hers was just an ordinary common sense approach, but I have found common sense is a very rare quality.

As the years progressed, I came to rely on her more and more. When we bought several other publications and were then bought over ourselves, I became Managing Editor and that resulted in all kinds of management meetings and other engagements. More and more I was absent from my desk.

But while Siobhan took on much of the burden not once did she attempt to undermine me. The opposite in fact. She ensured that I knew everything that had happened while I was away, and always gave me the right steer so that I didn't put my big feet unthinkingly into a boiling pot. She was irreplaceable in so, so many ways.

That she too was to be diagnosed with cancer just a few years after Domhnall was an awful blow. Married by this stage, she was the mother of four beautiful children whom she absolutely adored. They were her life. And she had great ambitions for them, wanting them to live the best lives possible.

It is beyond tragedy that she didn't get to see them achieve that very ambition, but I know she would be extremely proud of them were she alive today.

One person I also owed a lot to was the Reader – the person who read the typed copy for spelling mistakes – when I joined the Journal, Billy McLaughlin. The fact that he ended up as a reader despite having little formal education was a fair indicator of just how intelligent he was. And I was to benefit greatly from that intelligence.

In my early days in the Editor's Chair, I sometimes naively took risks, often allowing dodgy copy to slip through. A couple of hours later there would be a knock on by door and Billy could come in with copy stuck up his jumper – he didn't want to be seen undermining or questioning the Editor's authority – asking me if I was sure I was allowing this or that to appear in the paper. I developed a simple rule, if Billy queried it then I dropped it. God knows how many libel cases he saved me from in those early days.

Joe Martin, the head of page make-up, was another gem. He could be as crotchety as bedamned but had a heart of gold. Many were the occasions he got me out of a tight spot in the early days.

Around the table out on the production floor at break time could be hilarious. Around the table would sit Joe, Newell McBride, Willie O'Connell and assorted others.

Newell was unusual in Derry in those days in that he was a Protestant who had converted to Catholicism when he married. He could be absolutely hilarious. He used to bemoan the fact that he had changed religion by asking why everything that was fun in life was, according to the Catholic Church, a sin. Sex was a sin. Gambling was a sin. Going out with other women – same. One of his most famous quips was about the ferocious appetite of a certain footballer who was known to be carrying a few pounds. Newell's considered opinion that the best way to get him to lose weight would be to paint a chicken on the ball, and he would then run after it all day!

Willie O'Connell was an SDLP councillor who was later to serve as Mayor of the city. He was a serious man, a nice man, and a decent man. And he was to prove a very useful source of information on many occasions.

One of the characters of note too was John Curran. He had fingers that were almost the length of spaghetti straws and his ability to type copy was, quite literally, world class. He sat slouched in his computer chair, fingers going like Usain Bolt hurtling down a track and by the end of the day he produced more finished copy than, probably, the combined staff in that department. He was highly intelligent too, his finished product usually having very few mistakes or typos. It was amazing what he could do.

These days only two people from the Editorial Department of my era remain, Sean McLaughlin and Michael Wilson. They are two good newspaper men who are still hanging in there. All the production staff have long gone.

EUROPE'S BIGGEST OPEN-AIR PRISON

In 1981 the west bank of Derry was the biggest open prison in Europe. Of that there was no doubt. There were British Army/RUC checkpoints at all main entries and exits with the small, rural roads that criss-crossed into Donegal sealed off with huge concrete bollards wrapped in barbed wire.

The city centre too had military installations at all key strategic points. It was not uncommon to get stopped two or three times a day in vehicle spot checks which could hold traffic up for anything from five minutes to a couple hours depending on the capriciousness of those involved.

And just to make the already flammable mix so much more combustible the hunger strikes were in full flow.

All the streetlights in the city centre had been shot out so there was total darkness at night, black flags flew from most houses on the west bank, graffiti supporting the hunger strikers was all pervasive, hardly a gable wall was missed out, and the tension was palpable.

I was only in the Journal a couple of weeks before I began to wonder if I had made the right move. The strife outside was one thing but I wasn't too sure about what was going on inside. From the outset I found the Editor, Frank Curran, civil enough but it would be pushing it to describe his welcome as warm. He was wary of my appointment. With hindsight, he had a point.

I was only in situ as Chief Reporter a short time – about three weeks - when Curran decided to take holidays leaving me in charge. I was a bag of nerves. The unwritten conventions of reporting the Troubles were a minefield. The British Army did not murder IRA volunteers, they killed them. But the Brits insisted when the IRA killed a British soldier that was murder. Republicans saw it the other way round.

The legalities were also a minefield. There were accusations of RUC and security force brutalities and you had to take the risk that various individuals wouldn't sue. You took the chance on the basis that anyone who did would be really putting their head above the parapet which would, most likely, make them an IRA target.

And there was always the question of how much credence could you/should you give to alleged paramilitaries giving coded messages about bombing and shooting incidents – complete with recognised passwords – over the phone?

Would you find out later you had been sold a total dummy, that it was some fellas in a bar having a laugh? Or if you discredited it and a bomb went off, were you responsible for the carnage that would possibly ensue?

To make matters worse, I didn't even know the names of some of the key staff, and I certainly didn't know the technical end of newspaper production. It was a lot more complex then than it is now; hi-tech computers and page make-up on screen has ensured no worries in regard to copy. Back then it was often wholly dependent on the experienced eye of the Editor to gauge how many columns of news were available. And I had no experience.

Already more than a bit nervous about the Monday coming up, just to really pour it on, the IRA shot dead the Belfast MP, Rev Robert Bradford on the Saturday (Nov 14th, 1981). The killing caused absolute mayhem in the unionist community. Bradford was a hard-line politician and a hard-line religious whose views suggested it was morally okay to use lethal force against those rebelling against the State. This was interpreted in the nationalist communities in the North as saying it was okay for the security forces to shoot Catholics who were protesting against the State.

Following the killing of the MP, the firebrand preacher Ian Paisley and others called for a day of protest on the Monday to make their anger known. The North was to be closed down.

The RUC in Derry didn't cover themselves in glory that day (Monday, Nov 16, '81) siding very clearly with the unionist community in totally disrupting the life of the city. The then mayor of Derry, SDLP councillor, Joe Fegan, known to be the most moderate of people, rang me in mid-afternoon to say that police officers were blocking the Craigavon Bridge preventing children from the east bank of the Foyle who had been going to school on the west bank from getting home. When confronted they had been both abusive and sectarian in some of their comments. He issued a very strong statement condemning the actions of those officers. I splashed that as the lead, and we carried a lot of the reaction to the events in the inside pages.

Going into work on the Tuesday, the proprietor 'Old Frank' McCarroll – he had a son 'Young Frank' – came into the Editor's office and told me it was the best paper the Journal had produced in a very long time and that I should be proud of myself. Colm, the General Manager, shook my hand and laughingly suggested Curran should take holidays more often. Far from being the disaster I had feared it turned out that issue was to rapidly change my Journal career.

While an absolutely superb journalist and writer, I found Frank's editorial decision-making hit or miss. Despite Derry being of world importance in news terms at that time he sometimes seemed oblivious to what was going on around him.

A simple example comes to mind. When Pope John Paul II was the victim of an attempted assassination in Rome he made that the lead story. What was the point? Where was the local angle, and how could a local paper add anything to a story covered by just about every major television and news outlet in the world three days earlier?

He was idiosyncratic. One day he went over to the bank a few hundred yards from the Journal building on Buncrana Rd, ran into a stray pack of dogs roaming the area and came back and was livid. He told a reporter to contact the RSPCA to get a comment, get a councillor to condemn the city's stray dogs and proceeded to make it not only the lead story but he also wrote the editorial on the subject and had a letter with a fictitious name appear on the Letters Page. It was a bit over the top.

His coverage of the Hunger Strikes of 1981 had me even more confused. This was a seminal event in Irish history but if you are looking for narrative and context in the Derry Journal of that time you might be a tad disappointed. In May 1981 Derry INLA man Patsy O'Hara's death was a global event, the fourth hunger striker to die in Long Kesh. The tension of the hunger strikes was building to a terrible crescendo. Across the world the phenomenon of IRA men starving themselves to death in political protest was at its apex yet when O'Hara passed on the Derry Journal's coverage was hardly comprehensive.

The death of a second INLA man, Mickey Devine, shortly after I joined the paper in August of the same year didn't get anything like the comprehensive coverage I felt it deserved. What little coverage it did get, I was responsible for but it's not something I would win awards for.

But I later learned that the final straw for the proprietors was a more straightforward incident. In late October/early November of 1981 Paddy Harte, the long serving Fine Gael TD in Donegal, rang one Thursday afternoon to say he was going to New York to rescue a young Donegal girl who had joined a cult, the Moonies. He was, he said, going on behalf of the girl's distraught parents.

He told me it was exclusive to the 'Journal'.

I thought it would make the lead as, even in national terms, it was a pretty important story. I wrote it up, left it on the 'In Copy' basket on Curran's desk expecting that he would do the usual - sub it, mark a heading size and send it out to the production staff to type up for the next day's paper. As I finished early that particular night, I thought nothing more about it.

On the Friday I was off but bought the paper at the local newsagent's and was shocked to find the story hadn't appeared at all. I was definitely annoyed about it but thought nothing more of it. Editors are in charge, and if Frank had decided not to use it that was his prerogative.

What I didn't know was that just about the time I was having this inner dialogue with myself one of the senior advertising staff had occasion to leave something in Frank's office on the Friday morning. While in the office something must have caught his eye so out of curiosity he lifted the story still on top of the 'In-Copy' basket and started to read it. Colm McCarroll came in, apparently, about the same time and was shown the story, and then a whole inquest got underway why a weak lead story – if I recall correctly, it was about communal heating in houses in the Bogside - had appeared when there was a much better story sitting on Frank's desk.

Later that morning the home phone rang, and I was quizzed by Colm when I had written the story, when I had left it on Frank's desk etc. To put it mildly, he was not happy.

I would think Frank hadn't deliberately spiked the story, he simply had a rule that copy that arrived after 4 pm didn't make it into the next day's paper unless it was a double shooting or whatever. He liked getting finished early on Thursday nights.

By this stage he and the directors were on a collision course over issues that didn't concern me, and maybe he should have pulled back for his own sake. However just a couple of weeks later when he got engaged in a full-blown row about, of all things, using photographs of Derry Feis competitors, things really did explode.

The exact details escape me now but as far as I recall the rule was that only 'firsts' were photographed at the Feis. And for good reason. This was one of the biggest feiseanna in Ireland with up to 7,000 competitors participating, and there was no way we could take everyone's picture.

The catalyst for this row was a lady whose daughter had not got a first was really annoyed, wanting to know why it had to be firsts only? Was the Journal not being elitist? In the spirit of inclusiveness, she argued that it was the participating that counted, that it should be open to all. It shouldn't all be about coming first.

She had a point. But the problem was, as I have already pointed out, if we had followed her logic and published every picture taken it would have required the exclusion of all other photographic coverage for at least six weeks to two months..

However, her point that taking part was every bit as important as winning was reasonable as well. And one of the directors held strongly that the firsts only policy was misguided.

Whatever the rights or wrongs of the policy, Frank was of the opinion that as Editor what appeared should be his call, and he considered what was happening direct interference. Angry words were exchanged. He got really annoyed, went home to St John's Park, just across the street from the Journal offices, and when he came in the next morning, he informed management he would be resigning.

That very same day I was sitting at my desk when my phone rang: 'Come into my office – NOW!' said Colm McCarroll. It was clear something big had come up.

When I got there, he was off his seat: 'Frank has just been in with the old man. He's offered his resignation, and my dad has accepted it.'

He added, somewhat rhetorically, 'You fancy being the next Editor?'

I had just turned 28 and here I was, less than three months in the door, being offered the editorship of one of world's oldest newspapers, a paper with a major role in one of the most intractable conflicts, and a paper more successful in financial terms than many of the nationals. It was a dream come true, things like this didn't happen to people like me.

Needless to say, I was told to keep my mouth shut, that there were formalities to be addressed and sorted out. I went home and told Rosie, but I never told another soul. It was a strange time.

As the weeks passed, I almost thought they had changed their minds because absolutely nothing happened. I really thought there was a problem. Christmas came and went and January '82 was speeding along and still nothing.

Then on Wednesday, January 13th Colm came into the reporter's office, signalled to me with an almost imperceptible nod and headed directly into Frank Curran's office. About two minutes later the two of them walked out heading to Frank McCarroll's office.

This behaviour was so unusual the Editorial room was agog and soon out on the production floor there were staff gathering to gossip. The whole building knew something big was happening. Knowing what was happening I kept my head down and said nothing.

Eventually, Frank Curran came down the narrow corridor that then ran between the reporters' office and the production floor, he stared straight at me through the large glass partition for a few seconds with a strange expression before pulling the door on to the production area without coming near me. I knew he was in a kind of shock. I can only presume again that he had thought they had decided by that stage to ignore his resignation.

In fairness to both Frank and the McCarrolls, the whole transition was actually handled with considerable tact and diplomacy, and they continued to do business together for another 25 years, with Frank contributing to both the Journal and then the Derry News well into his eighties. Importantly, it allowed Frank to return to his real love - writing. And within five years of stepping down as editor he had authored two seminal histories, *Derry: Countdown to Disaster* and *The Derry City Story: 1928-1986.*

But I wasn't thinking any of this as events were unfolding.

It was the longest two minutes in history until Colm came into the Reporters' Room and asked, 'Pat, can we see you for a couple of minutes?'

On entering Mr. McCarroll Snr's office he immediately stuck out his hand and offered me the job.

There were two things he made clear. Firstly, they would not interfere with me doing my job. 'Isn't that right, Colm?', he added, looking at his son. I should maybe have read more into that one at the time.

He also said one other thing: 'Pat, there are hundreds of teachers in this area, hundreds of policemen, hundreds of nurses, but there is only one Editor of the Derry Journal. That will be you.'

What he was telling me in his kindly way was not to bring any disrepute on a paper he had spent his life protecting and building.

This was the day that a whole new life began for me.

THE IMPORTANCE OF THE 'LOCAL RAG'

One aspect of the local paper that is often overlooked was its role in connecting and communicating with the Irish diaspora. Like The Tuam Herald, The Donegal Democrat or The Kilkenny People, copies of the Derry Journal would have been sent all over the world to emigrants in America, Australia, Canada, England and elsewhere.

This was brought home to me one day when I looked at the circulation figures for Inishowen. I became aware that we were selling far more papers there than there were households, and I was stumped why this would be so. It was only when someone explained that in many houses they bought two Journals on a Friday – one for themselves, one for the son or daughter who had emigrated – that the mystery of sales figures was explained.

The local paper was an important link to home as in the era before hi-tech it was only there some lad working on a site in Birmingham or Brisbane would see the wedding photograph of an ex-girlfriend, learn of the death of a neighbour, or read the court case of an old school pal. I was only too aware of the role of the paper in this regard as for years my mother sent the Derry Journal to her friend Annie McMenamin on Long Island. Annie had emigrated in 1948 and was still getting copies of the local paper into the 1980s.

In many ways papers were part of the cementing of society in that it was a medium of keeping everyone up to speed with what was happening.

Eamonn McCann's book *War in an Irish Town* gives a brilliant account of the role the 'Journal' played in forming opinions in Derry or more specifically, nationalist/Catholic Derry.

For years Dr. Neil Farren had been the unofficial, unelected leader of the Catholic Community in Derry, both politically and spiritually. A somewhat pompous little man he had been an academic who had been moved from his role as President of St Columb's College to the bishopric, and there were those who claimed he never lost the knack of talking down to adults as if they were his students.

When I arrived Dr Edward Daly was Bishop of Derry. He was a cleric of very different disposition and character, but Farren's legacy was still very much in evidence.

The famous image of the young Fr. Daly waving a blood-stained handkerchief as men behind carried the body of Jackie Duddy, the first young man to be shot on Bloody Sunday in 1972, had brought him to worldwide prominence. Farren, who was not a good media performer, either got or allowed Daly to do all the media interviews and it was he who soon 'spoke' for the Catholics of Derry.

Edward Daly was a decent man in every sense of the word, trying to do an almost impossible job in very difficult circumstances. Personally, I found him much more liberal in private than some of his more public pronouncements. He was also a deeply humane man who felt the suffering of the people at a profound level.

There was an old story that three IRA members were in the grounds of St Eugene's Cathedral when Bishop Daly came out and asked them what they were doing. On learning they were planning to attack and kill members of a British army patrol he told them to leave the sacred ground of a church.

'Fuck away off, Bishop,' said one agitated young man.

Later that evening that young man was shot in the leg as punishment. Apparently, for the good Catholic IRA leaders it was not acceptable behaviour for a volunteer to tell a bishop to fuck off.

While this might be an apocryphal story there is more than a little bit of truth in it.

For example, Martin McGuinness's parents were deeply religious people, almost daily communicants. McGuinness himself would have been a child any Catholic parent would have been proud of – didn't drink, didn't smoke, absolutely no scandal about his private life, well mannered, polite and, while quiet, was very affable.

In the early days I used to wonder about the people of Derry's loyalty to the paper; that if it was in the 'Journal' that was it, it was gospel. Coming from a rural county of Donegal I used to laugh to myself when Derry people suggested to me, they were much more cosmopolitan, more sophisticated. I didn't buy it. In all my years in Donegal I don't think the Catholic bishop of Raphoe ever had a lead story. In all my years in Derry the Bishop of Derry was rarely off the front page.

Paradoxically, Derry should have been much different. The city had been used as a base by the Americans during World War II and they brought with them attitudes and influences on religious and sexual liberty that certainly were different to the existing mores in the city. The old maxim 'one Yank and they are down' - a ribald reference to the underwear of young ladies who went out with the servicemen during that era - was a commonly heard comment. The 'oldest profession' was rife too with any number of women making a living 'on the boats'; that was something never mentioned publicly but privately acknowledged.

I recall too one morning at Mass in Pennybурн Church the priest in his homily stating that there were too many young married men who thought they were still single. He bemoaned the level of casual sexual activity which, he said, was leading to wholesale marriage breakdown.

But the guys who were committing adultery on a Saturday night were probably up for communion with their wives and children on a Sunday morning.

So, whilst on one hand there were bombings, shootings, gambling and affairs but there was also massive observance for the main religious traditions in the city and respect for the clergy that served these communities. It was a very conflicted society.

MY ROLE IN THE PEACE PROCESS

In the Journal, unlike the big national papers, we didn't have the luxury of working ahead. The nationals had big staffs considering layout, choosing headlines, styling and designing features and pages. Each edition of our publication was stand-alone. Once one paper was finished, we started from scratch on the next.

And that meant Thursdays for the big paper, the broadsheet, was hell for leather. Fourteen to fifteen-hour shifts were the norm, and it was full-on for those fourteen to fifteen hours.

So, one day in late 1993 when I got a call from Kathleen Green who was the American Consul in Belfast, asking me to meet someone she was bringing to Derry on a Thursday, I declined. I hardly had time for a cup of coffee so why would I be bothered to entertain some Yank who wanted a chat? She was very insistent, but I still said no.

About a day later she rang again and was almost pleading that it would only take fifteen minutes – that we could do it over my lunch hour or whatever. She was a nice woman and I cottoned on that it was important for her so I, eventually, relented.

On the Thursday sure enough, in she arrived with this American who looked straight out of central casting – tall, tanned, blond, beefy, teeth that you could see your reflection in and wearing the white raincoat that all US government types seemed to be issued with.

He was friendly, and clearly well briefed. I was, I recall, preoccupied with a number of stories we were urgently following up and not initially paying a lot of attention.

The fifteen minutes originally sought went on for an hour and half and I, quite literally, had to ask them to leave. As I was so far behind I hadn't the time to think any more of it.

The following Monday Martin McGuinness was down for his usual visit and just as he was about to leave I remarked, 'By the way, there was a big Yank in here on Thursday asking a lot of questions about you.'

Martin then asked me who he was, and when I gave him the man's name – which I now totally forget - he immediately turned back, sat down and asked me what I had told him. And I recall, unusually for Martin, he seemed a wee bit agitated.

I gave a brief outline of my discussions with the American and then Martin stated the guy I had met was a senior official from the State Department, and that he was a 'spook' of some kind. How he knew this I don't know. He also told me to keep it to myself but under-cover negotiations were ongoing as to whether Bill Clinton would grant Gerry Adams and himself visas to visit the States. They had been barred from visiting by various US administrations on the basis of alleged IRA activities.

No wonder it was sensitive. This was big time politics at play.

What actually happened was I got time to reflect on the week while sitting at home over the weekend. I started to ruminate on my discussions with the American. It was obvious I had missed something in my haste to get them out of my hair. It came to me that he had asked a lot of personal questions, rather than political ones. What type of person Martin was? Would I trust him? Had he ever broken his word to me?

That was why I mentioned it to Martin that day, that it had struck me as odd. Had I not been distracted I should have realised he was looking for some kind of character reference for McGuinness. It really was that obvious.

And it was Martin's uncharacteristic response that had given the game away.

Clinton was taking a big risk granting the Republican leadership entry into the States, it would be seen as giving them legitimacy and it was certain to enrage the Brits – which it did. Therefore, before annoying the crap out of their old ally, the one the British liked to describe as 'our special relationship' - the Americans were out gathering evidence on which they could make their decision.

It's doubtful if the Irish government was overjoyed at the prospect of the two main men in the Republican Movement getting star treatment in the States either. So, it was a major diplomatic move by the Clinton administration, something they didn't want blowing up in their face.

This visit by the US duo was an important part of that decision-making process.

McGuinness and Adams did eventually get to go visit the States. I presume there were strict conditions attached and agreed with them at the outset. For the Americans it was then a question of checking them out, and once they had satisfied that all avenues had been explored it was green for go.

I suppose I could say that was my contribution to the peace process. Gerry Adams and Martin McGuinness got their visas.

POWER AND INFLUENCE

I was about ready to leave the house one morning to take the kids to school, when the press officer for the Western Health Trust, based at Altnagelvin, rang. He was clearly in a panic. 'Pat, what is this morning's lead story?'

Seeing that it was an unusual request to be getting at 8.45am I told him.

It was only too obvious that he hadn't seen the paper and as, officially, he didn't start work until 9am, I wondered what was going on.

'The Minister is going mad, and my boss is panicking,' he explained.

The Minister being referred to was Richard Needham and he was an unusual type of politician. There was some story about health cuts which was critical of the Minister, and he was enraged. What was surprising was that Needham in Belfast had not only got access to but had also read the Journal beforc any of the health officials in Derry.

But I knew he was that type of minister. He liked to be on top of things.

A couple of months earlier I had my first encounter with him. Reporter Siobhan McEleney had been at a press conference in the city centre shortly after his appointment and it had been an experience for her. Not a particularly good experience!

The previous week Needham had made a big speech where he wanted to outline his credentials as a minister who would work for everyone, that he understood why people west of the Bann had a chip on their shoulder. It was a boilerplate speech, one that had often been heard before.

I wasn't aware that in the Friday edition Frank Curran, who wrote the leaders then, had dismissed his comments along the lines that he would be just another British politician saying all the right things but doing nothing concrete – that he would be just another rotating minister who would talk the talk but not walk the walk.

At the press conference Needham publicly asked if a representative from the Derry Journal was present, and when Siobhan put up her hand, he berated her from the lectern for the coverage in the weekend paper. When she arrived back at the office, she came straight into me and said Needham had demanded my direct line number and that he would be ringing me to complain. I thought 'yeah right, a British minister is going to ring me' and put it out of my head.

Ten minutes later the phone rang. It was Needham. And he wasn't happy.

How dare I describe him as just another talking shop? Did I know anything about him? Cheap jibes about someone just weeks in the job were despicable. He should be judged at the end of his term, not the start.

I could see why he had become a politician. I didn't get a word in edgeways. When he finally took a break to get some air back in his lungs, I told him we would gladly apologise at that time - at the end of his sojourn here - if he delivered for Derry. It didn't happen.

One other example of the Journal's influence was a bit more surreal. I don't know how I came to see it but as I looked out my window one afternoon, I was struck by a purple Porsche being driven in our front gate. No one in Derry, as far as I was aware, had a purple car, never mind a purple Porsche. About five minutes later Reception called to say there was a man in the front office who wanted to speak to me for two minutes.

In he came in his fine suit and with a cut-glass accent to match. He even addressed me as Mr McArt without us never having met.

He then proceeded to tell me that I should be careful what headlines we put in the paper. That what appeared could affect the big decisions under consideration by possible investors. He advised that before industrialists or corporations made decisions about locations, they scoped out all possible information as to what the local conditions were. This included a comprehensive review of the local media.

And then he stated: 'I was in the Australian Parliament in Canberra less than a month ago. All I am saying to you is that the Derry Journal was very much up front in our discussions.'

To this day I don't know what project was being discussed in Canberra or where the Journal came in on those discussions, but there you go.

Of course, it is worth recording here that Needham's outspokenness was to catch up on him. Travelling in his official car in November 1990 he called his wife on the phone and when discussing Mrs Thatcher's problems with her party he remarked: 'I wish that cow would resign.'

'An unnamed paramilitary group', that is how it was described, had been scanning his outgoing calls and recorded it, sending a copy to a Belfast news agency. Needham had to apologise. Thatcher accepted it, but his career hit a serious speed bump.

NO MORE JOURNALISTS....

I remember from my youth Muddy Waters having a hit song with 'I got my Mojo working'. I was never quite sure what his 'mojo' was. I had all but forgotten the word until nearly forty years later I'm sitting in the Journal's brand new hi-tech, hi-spec office block when I hear the word again.

Sitting in front of me is this bright young Englishman telling me how the reporter of 2013 is not a journalist anymore; he/she is a 'content gatherer'. That was news to me. He tells too of the need to be 'multi-skilled' in technology.

Now it's no longer a question of writing a report for the next edition of the paper, there is also an onus to get it on the web, give 'lead ins' about the story on Twitter and Facebook and a video interview of the main players then to be posted on the net in conjunction with publication for, as he put it, 'the complete package'.

In short, we should, he explained, be a 'mojo'– a mobile journalist.

For me the light first came on in my brain that the old ways were dying in one eureka moment in the early 1990s. It was David Connolly who provided that moment.

Connolly, our Australian correspondent, would send on copy and photographs from around the continent about five or six times a year. He had a link up of Derry people in places like Sydney, Perth, Adelaide etc.

There was a lot of work involved. He would have to physically go to the events, take photos, write up his story, come home, take the film to the chemists, get negatives, go back for the developed photos, write out captions, Sellotape those captions on to the back of the photos, get a big envelope, go to the post office, get a stamp and post it all off to me. And it took about ten days to get to Derry.

One day he rang from his home in Melbourne telling me he had become a grandfather for the first time. Not only that but he had, he informed me, got himself a computer and he was sending me a photo electronically to my recently installed computer. Ten minutes later I saw an email with an attachment – he had sent on a photograph of his new grandchild taken less than 30 minutes earlier. You didn't need to be a visionary to see what was coming down the track.

As I have mentioned previously, Frank Curran was an institution in the journal, serving his entire career there. Now in the twilight of his long career he loved telling stories of the old days.

One of his favourites was telling of heading off to cover Buncrana court on a July day. The mode of transport was a Lough Swilly bus which left Derry at around 9 a.m. and once out of the city the option of a return was not available until late in the evening. On this particular day he was referring to, it being a fine morning Frank decided to take his tennis racquet and shoes as he knew the court - the law one - would probably finish early and he could get a quick game in before catching the last bus home.In he lands at court, puts the tennis gear under the seat and starts taking down the notes. Around lunch time it's all over and as Frank is about to leave the judge calls him over.

Judge Louis Walsh: 'Are you going for a game of tennis, Frank?'

Frank: 'I am, indeed, Louis. But I have these reports to do so it'll be a while.

Judge Walsh: 'Don't worry about the court. I'll sort that out.'

When Frank came back three or four hours later each case had been typed up neatly, complete with details of witness statements, defendants' pleas and names and addresses, and judges' comments. Walsh had been a journalist in an earlier life and was totally conversant with the style of local newspaper court reporting and provided Frank with spotless copy ready to insert straight on to the page.

The added benefit was, I suppose, no one was going to sue for erroneous reporting, not when a judge would back up the report as being 'fair and accurate'.

One fount of old stories was the former Editor of the Donegal People's Press, John McIntyre. One of his favourites was of a crotchety old judge on the Donegal Circuit in the 1950s, Mr Justice O'Uadaigh.

One day at a sitting in Newtowncunnigham an old farmer was in the witness box and much to the annoyance of the judge he kept chewing gum. O'Uadaigh tapped the court clerk, Liam McGoldrick on the shoulder and told him: 'Tell that man to stop masticating.'

McGoldrick stood up and shouted out to the witness: 'The judge says to take your hands out of your pockets...'

One hilarious court report in Letterkenny in the 1970s told of how some of the town's best known, most respected citizens were found drinking out of hours in a well-known hotel on the Main Street. Someone had tipped the password to get into the session to the local Garda Sergeant who accompanied by a couple of fine men raided the shindig only to see a whole host of the late drinkers run for the stairs.

The race then began to find the miscreants before they got out back doors, windows etc. Eventually two well-known sports stars were found hiding in a closet in the bridal suite. When the full details came out - half of which were never made public in court - it was the talk of the town for weeks, and the ribald jokes were flying for years.

What was not known was that the man who got the report, Sean Curran, had missed court that day. However, the local Garda superintendent enjoyed the case so much he wanted to share the craic with the population at large and passed the file to Sean who printed it in full.

That would never happen now. Everyone is way too careful.

The human side of reporting was witnessed when one young reporter nearly got himself jailed for contempt in the early 1970s. Justice Michael Larkin had listened to a case for about 20 minutes when he declared he had heard enough and was going to convict the defendant. An enraged young reporter, whose blushes need sparing, stood up and asked: 'How did you reach that conclusion?' It took the calming presence of veteran reporter, Jackie Geelan, to cool the judge down and let the young lad away with a warning to keep his mouth shut in court in future.

Indeed, for many years I was a court reporter covering Larkin's beat and to say he was idiosyncratic would be putting it very mildly. Despite being a Labour Party nominee to the bench he was an arch conservative who saw things pretty much in black and white. He would snap at ill-dressed defendants – 'Take your hat off in court' – but tended to fawn over well-dressed professional types. He lived in a big house outside Letterkenny and, on occasions, would invite John McIntyre out to dinner where his wife would present six-course meals in the grand drawing room.

He hated courts in Gweedore. And for good reason. They were held in a glorified chicken shed in Bunbeg. One day we arrived and the place wasn't ready because someone had forgotten to clean it out. He was fuming, threatening to cancel the court until it was pointed out to him that a lot of busy people had been summoned to appear there and he was not doing them any favours

And Larkin didn't like being cold either. He used to ensure on the cold winter days, of which there were many, the oil heater was placed beside his bench and to hell with the rest of us.

But the thing was that the officers of the court and the judiciary in the South were mostly on good terms with the media. Judges would, almost automatically, hand down the charge sheets and summons so that reporters could get names and addresses. It was not uncommon either for a cop, a solicitor or even a judge

- that happened to me more than once - to tip you off that there was a big case coming up and not to miss it by heading out for a cup of coffee or whatever.

Nowadays reporters write to predetermined shapes on pages. This ensures court and council reports often have little of the colour of the proceedings, mainly sticking to key facts and decisions. That colour was often what gave newspapers the edge over the broadcast and social media, got people talking over the hedges or in the pubs.

It is also telling that reporters are now described as 'content-gatherers' not journalists – this speaks volumes as the priority is not news but on filling a particular specified space. Whether the story is so good it deserves double the particular space is not a consideration.

And years back the Editor was key to pagination in that he – it was usually he back then – would decide on the size of the paper. Now, it's the advertising department. That tells you all you need to know about where the power in newspapers now lies.

Finally, it is beyond question that modern technology has made a lot of newspapers seem slow and out of touch in a high-speed world and this is hitting circulations on a massive scale. When you can read on screen what the Taoiseach or the Secretary of State has said ten minutes after they have said it you hardly feel the need to buy a paper.

But a good paper with good writers doing reportage and analysis has a role to play so it could be argued many of the wounds in regard to declining circulations have been self-inflicted by big media conglomerates more interested in profits than in producing quality newspapers. There are still people willing to buy a paper if they are getting value for money but finding a paper where news is secondary and where there are full page adverts on pages 3,5, 7 and on the centre spread etc is not exactly an inducement to hand over a couple of hard-earned quid.

THE BRITS COME A-CALLING

One day I got a call from a British army press officer I had got to know asking would I meet him the following day at a well-known restaurant in the Waterside area. I was intrigued by what seemed urgent to him, so I agreed. He was a genuinely nice bloke who had one of those double-barrelled type names, something like Alistair Formby-Smyth. And he looked and sounded like he should be married into minor royalty.

Usually, these dinners were attended by a number of other officers, and it was all on the credit card, but this time I noted that 'Alastair' was paying everything out of his own pocket. So, I asked him what was so urgent?

The story went that every Tuesday and Friday morning when he arrived at his desk the colonel, his boss, had already gone through every story in the Journal and ringed in red comments where the behaviour of British troops was mentioned. He not only expected Alastair to know about them but to have a response.

Alastair asked: 'Pat, I know it's not your job but any chance you could tip me off when stories about our boys are appearing? It would make my life a lot easier.'

That simple episode told me that the British did take their PR seriously, that they wanted to control how they were portrayed. They liked the message to go out that they were the honest brokers who were piggy-in-the-middle. It wasn't true, but that was the game they wanted to play.

I have to admit that I found the British army types fascinating. One day I was invited over to Ebrington Barracks where the colonel turned out to be a real extrovert. He wasn't half slugging the wine into him as we had dinner, He suddenly asked: 'Tell me something, Pat – do you believe Bloody Sunday was a cock-up or a conspiracy, that we had it all planned beforehand?'

I responded that the evidence suggested to me there was indeed planning so therefore I viewed it as a deliberate, planned action designed to teach the nationalist community in Derry a hard lesson.

He responded: 'I firmly believe it was a total cock-up. You people (nationalist community) think the British army is this well-oiled, disciplined, strategic thinking unit. Let me tell you, it's far from it. Given half a chance we can fuck-up anything. And we fucked up big time that day.'

I didn't believe it then and I don't believe it now, but I have no doubt he believed it.

On another occasion I was invited up to the British army's HQ in Belfast and a somewhat heated discussion arose about the role of the UDR. I suggested they are little more than thugs in uniform, loyalists handed guns by the British government under the guise of security. That the nationalist community could give chapter and verse of naked sectarianism, of assaults right up to murders.

In one barracks alone, Drumadd, over the years quite a few UDR personnel had been charged with multiple murders or attempted murders. And that was only when the authorities had little choice but to do so.

I expected little support so was surprised when one man, a major, responded: 'I agree totally.' Turned out his father was from Armagh and his mother was a Cork woman. His name badge said 'Ryan'.

And then there was the senior officer who told me that if he lived in the North, he would join the IRA. I went 'What?' A British army officer supporting the actions of the IRA?

'I would have joined the IRA. Definitely. If I was a Catholic in this place, I wouldn't have put up with the bigotry and the sectarianism. Listening to that bigot (Paisley) would enrage me.'

Perhaps the oddest comment was from a man in uniform who told me he was a pacifist, that his years in the army had taught him there had to be a better way. Sitting surrounded by guns, heavily armoured vehicles and uniformed personnel everywhere I thought it was a strange place for a pacifist to find himself.

Of course, the RUC too was keen to get its point of view across too. Over the years there was a ragbag of personnel, some great, some bloody awful.

One I recall was so laconic you'd swear he was half asleep. When reporters would ring him up to check if there were any overnight incidents, he would rhyme it off like a laundry list.

One morning, according to a reporter, he started off as usual: 'Car burned out in Shantallow, kneecapping in the Bogside, petrol bombs thrown at army patrol in the Waterside, a body found .....'

The thought didn't seem to occur to him that a body found should have been first on the list, the main priority.

As well as the securocrats we also had regular visits from British politicians. On one occasion the Secretary of State, Sir Patrick Mayhew came visiting. He was from the old patrician school – tall, cut-glass accent and very polite. He insisted I join him for dinner in the White Horse Hotel at Eglinton, and that

I travel in his official car. I was thinking to myself if I were seen, my street cred with the Shinners was shot.

One of his flunkeys made a mistake too in that he left a briefing document behind which gave a run-down on me – who I was, where I was from, and other background details. In fairness to them I couldn't see anything damaging to me in it. Like a lot of other things, I should have held onto it for posterity sake, but it too disappeared into some hiding hole never to be seen again.

I don't know how I became friendly with Dr. Brian Mawhinney when he was in the NIO but I did. He was unpopular with a lot of journalists because he was really sarcastic but we hit it off. He invited me to a number of private dinners in Hillsborough to meet the great and the good.

I think the fact that I made it clear on every occasion that I didn't buy the 'honest broker' version the British were peddling was why I kept getting invited. He wanted his guests to get an alternative opinion.

I also recall being invited to a dinner with Tom King on several occasions.

When he was Secretary of State he and the unionists had a big falling out after the Anglo-Irish Agreement and I got the distinct impression he actually detested them. This was based on a private conversation one night where he made clear that he found the attitude of some of them 'distinctly unhelpful'. Unfortunately, I didn't have a tape of that conversation which, had it been made public, would have done nothing to increase his standing within unionism.

One particular memory stands out, however.

I wasn't long in the Editor's chair when I was invited to Hillsborough Castle for the first time. It really is something else in terms of grandeur, the official royal family residence in Northern Ireland. It had much the same façade as St Eunan's College, my old secondary school! So, there I was sitting beside the British Secretary of State, having dinner in this grand room with uniformed servants serving the steaks and pouring the wine.

I remember clearly thinking if my old teachers and classmates at Eunan's could only see me now. It was a far cry from what I was used to, growing up in a council house in Letterkenny.

I was also only too aware how the Brits worked, a bit like the spider to the fly. No matter how many times I met these kinds of people I always reminded myself going in the door who I was and where I was from. It was a reality check not to get carried away. The fine wine and the old arm around the shoulder had seduced many over the years, and not for their good.

'THEM PEOPLE ARE MAD'

Journalists from all over the world used to visit, particularly in the early days. The vast majority were American, but I regularly had French and Italian and even the odd Swede dropping in.

An urban war in Europe in the 20th century was a never-ending source of fascination for them. What was it all about? Religious? Tribal? Cultural?

It was hard to explain that it was often a combination of all three.

What was more difficult to get across was that the simplistic portrayal in the British media of the warring factions in the North during the Troubles did no one any favours. The basic format was almost cartoonish – the Catholics were the mad rebels, the Protestants the red-faced bigots, the British Army the good guys. It was a paradigm the BBC were fond of, but I have long contended it was disgraceful that RTÉ should have adopted a narrative that pretty much echoed the British version. It was way more complex than that. But when RTÉ gave this shorthand version credence then it was accepted pretty much worldwide.

The result was a total distortion of the reality on the ground. It was left to papers like the Derry Journal to attempt to give balance to what was going on, often at the cost of being accused of being a 'republican rag' when exposing the often-wanton behaviour of the authorities and the security forces.

A very clear example of this is whilst everyone these days accepts that Bloody Sunday was the state killing totally innocent civilians back in 1972 the BBC and ITV were neutral in their language, describing the deaths as 'killings'. That was neutral on the side of the British authorities.

The Journal, on the other hand, from the outset used the term murder because that was what literally thousands of people locally had seen with their own eyes.

But this was often considered subversive. In a land where lies are pervasive, someone telling the truth is a danger. And we had a bit of a reputation.

Some years back a former senior civil servant in Dublin told me that one day he had a copy of the Journal on his desk when the Secretary of his department walked in. Noting the paper the guy remarked, 'What are you doing with that republican rag in here?'

The stereotyping of the communities in conflict helped cement the Dublin Four view, personified by the likes of Conor Cruise O'Brien in political circles and in the media by the likes of Gay Byrne – that 'they were all mad up there' and a plague on the whole lot of them. The outcome of this was it gave people in the South an excuse to wash their hands of it all.

How convenient was that?

They, basically, turned their backs on their fellow Catholic-nationalist Irish people who were forced to live under an artificially-created unionist state run by a single-party government for fifty years. To conform to the new disposition people who wanted a quiet life were expected to downplay – or even, on occasion, deny - their culture, their religion and their nationality.

Propaganda was the real battleground when the Troubles broke out. And with their long history of colonialism the Brits were masters at selling themselves as the good guys. It took republicans a long time to catch up in this regard, to realise there was more than one way of winning a war.

From the off the Brits knew where favourable public opinion could be bought. If there was raiding in the Creggan or on the Falls Road and women – it was always women – were angrily shouting into television cameras about their homes being wrecked and their men beaten up, on would come a Sandhurst officer type and in mellifluous tones tell how his men had had a jolly difficult job to do in the most trying of circumstances. If the bombing and shooting would stop, they wouldn't be raiding houses in the middle of the night. It was being done for these people's own good. Get those crazy terrorists to cut it out.

I saw first-hand how this worked in my teenage years, my mother frequently siding with the authority figure: 'They didn't get their houses raided for nothing,' she would opine. And she was far from alone.

Most people in the South seemed unaware that apart from the fifty years of unionist rule the police force, the RUC, was 93% Protestant and 100% unionist; the UDR was riddled with loyalist paramilitaries many of whom used its services to murder Catholics; that there was massive discrimination in housing and employment; emigration was destroying Catholic towns like Derry, Strabane and Newry; that the poorest wards in the North were all in Catholic areas.

And of course, most of the British army officers were frequently economical with the truth. Squaddies from the back streets of Glasgow or Liverpool, many of them coming from sink housing estates, trained up to be aggressive to fight in the British army, were thugs in uniform. Many of them were scared, most didn't want to be there and if the opportunity arose to, literally, put the boot in to arrested young fellas from the nationalist community, few resisted the temptation. But this type of thuggery was never acknowledged by the officers.

Typically, I recall many stories of abuse. And it took many forms.

One young female reporter told of being pulled out of bed in a state of undress during an early morning raid while soldiers standing by made crude and lewd remarks. She made mention too of seeing her father being pulled down the stairs by the hair. Homes were often maliciously wrecked during raids, good furniture ripped to shreds on the pretext soldiers were seeking to find guns and/or ammunition. Items such as sentimental ornaments and photos were often deliberately destroyed to cause maximum annoyance. It was small stuff, didn't make the headlines but it hardened attitudes on the ground. It was an everyday reality.

Of course, the British army people were careful not to alienate the professional classes, raids on the Culmore Road area a rarity. It should be said there were few of the professional classes – the doctors, the lawyers, the accountants – leading from the front in the Republican Movement. And the intelligence services would have been aware of that. The uprising in the nationalist community was pretty much a working-class movement.

But there were any number of paradoxes with regard to the type of people involved in the Republican movement. One man I recall meeting early in my career was a strong republican yet hated violence. I remember him well because he came to symbolise much of my own later confusion. Despite his hardman image Martin McGuinness loved to write poetry and was happiest away fishing in Donegal. Eamonn McDermott was a totally committed republican who could morally argue that using lethal force in war was justified but took exception to sexist remarks in the office. A guy I knew well and was, I am reliably informed, a top operator in the IRA's Active Service Unit I regularly met at Mass on Sundays and was, again I am told, a daily communicant.

These people didn't have two heads; they were people who found themselves in a time, a place and a situation that was way beyond their control. Had partition gone another way, we could have been talking about people in Cork, Kerry and Waterford.

Finally, I have to admit I think there was only one man I met over the years who was a psychopath, a guy who enjoyed violence. He made a couple of remarks that suggested that shooting someone was no big deal to him. And if the stories I had heard about him were true, it wasn't.

Years later when discussing someone totally different with Martin McGuinness I described one fella as a 'total psychopath' to which Martin replied with a smile: 'You know psychopaths have their uses.'

THE MOST POWERFUL MAN IN THE VILLAGE

Conor Cruise O'Brien, the academic and former Irish government minister, once said the Editor of the local newspaper was the most powerful man in the community because he could put your court case in the paper or, probably more importantly, leave it out. And that was real power.

Most local newspaper editors will tell you court cases were the bane of their lives. Probably still are.

Many people thought you could pay to keep them out and often there were attempts to bribe, punters throwing money on the desk. There were offers of foreign holidays, and threats of violence were not infrequent if things were not going the way the supplicant had anticipated. The number of times I was told, usually over the phone, I would get my teeth down the back of my throat I couldn't count.

It was not just difficulties for the Editor, in a small community they frequently caused problems for the extended family.

One Sunday night going out to a pub for a quiet drink in the village of Muff, quite close to where we lived in Derry turned into a bit of a nightmare. We hadn't been there long when over the low-level hum of noise came a loud voice: 'The Derry Journal. The fucking Derry Journal.... I wouldn't use it to wipe my arse.'

The place suddenly got a lot quieter.

My wife, noticing the beefy fella hanging around the bar doing the spouting, got a bit nervous and suggested we finish our drinks and leave. I thought to hell with it, I'm going nowhere.

Within seconds it started again. I genuinely didn't know what his problem was as I had never seen him before. Turned out the man's court case had been in the paper the Friday before where he had appeared in court for the non-payment of substantial sums of money.

While I hadn't a clue who he was, it was quite obvious he knew who I was. Fortunately, the proprietor of the bar made a point of going up to the gent in question and very firmly suggesting to him he keep his views on the Derry Journal to himself. We then left. It was a bit of a spoilt night out.

Years later I heard the story – my wife didn't tell me at the time – that my family didn't escape the fallout. There were a couple of incidents, but the most noteworthy was when my eldest son went to training when he was playing with his local team. On arrival at the clubhouse, he said hello to some people and was ignored, and as the evening wore on, he couldn't figure out why he was isolated; why no one would train with him. He was only 16 or 17 at the time. It wasn't a very nice thing to do to a decent young lad. He eventually discovered that a number of offspring of prominent members of the club had appeared in court after getting into some trouble at a nightclub in Letterkenny and that the court case had been in the paper that day. They couldn't get to me, so they did the next best thing.

The most extreme reaction came one day when this middle-aged man arrived in my office clearly in a very agitated state. He was a bit incoherent, and it took a while to get his story. Eventually the details emerged. Turned out he was a respectable married family man from the Inishowen area, a member of his church's ruling council. He had been found in a compromising position late at night in a lay-by in Derry by the RUC.

A woman would have been difficult to explain away to his family but the fact that he had been found with another man made it impossible.

He was in such a desperate plight he told me he had two farms and that he would sign one over there and then to me just so long as his case did not appear in the paper.

I did the usual stalling tactic, telling him that we had a rule of putting all cases in the paper and there was little I could do for him other than take his name and give it some consideration.

The man left but about two hours later I got a call from a man I knew well and had a lot of time for.

Says he: 'Pat, did you get a visit from (named person) this morning?'

I replied that I had.

'I don't know how I can put this any stronger,' says he, 'but if that case appears in Friday's Journal (named person) will be in the Foyle as soon as it does. Make no mistake about it – he will be destroyed. I'm not in any shape or form attempting blackmail here. I'm telling you the facts. Be aware of the consequences, that's what I am advising.'

I thought about it right-up to about ten minutes before publication. The primary thought that came to mind was who was I to play God. I didn't want to have anyone's death on my conscience. I decided to quietly drop it.

The only light side to this story was a few reporters who I had talked to and consulted with about the case used to ask me about cattle prices, suggesting I was now the silent partner in a big farm.

It was funny at the time....

At the other end of the extreme was a young fella who came in with his girlfriend. Originally too from Donegal he had been found supplying drugs to a number of people in clubs in Derry. His family would, he said, kill him and it would destroy their good name. Out came the usual sob story. His father was a well known figure in the community and it would ruin the family business if the story appeared in the paper, his mother wasn't well, he was going for a job interview the next day – just about every excuse was thrown in. Had he quit while ahead he would have been okay. But as he was leaving, he made a remark along the lines of, 'If you leave it out, I'll look after you', and I realised with that one remark – and the little sly look that accompanied it – he was a total con man. He was a drug pusher and had the mentality of a drug pusher.

The attitude of some people never ceased to amaze either. We had a reporter in a court in Donegal covering the case of a fatal accident where children had died. The driver was up on a dangerous driving charge. The reporter concerned rang up telling me the detail and describing the defendant's attitude in court in far from flattering terms. He had, according to the reporter, behaved like a thug on the day of the accident and the court had found his driving had led directly to the children's deaths.

Later that very day the defendant's father was put through. He was not the placatory type. He demanded that we not publish the case and if we did – and, he claimed, he had checked this out with his solicitor – he would sue us. His whole manner was intimidatory. He was more concerned about his son's image in the community than about the fact that he had killed two children. I put the case on the front page.

Mohammed Ali, the great heavyweight boxer, who when being challenged that in middle age he had changed his position on a number of issues from the days of his youth replied that it was, basically, an idiot who didn't learn from his or her experiences. I had plenty of experiences to learn from.

Early in my career I got the usual call that there were two women wanting to see me, but they were reluctant to give the receptionist any detail. That was the usual signal – court case.

In came the two women, mother and daughter, and I was embarrassed right away. I recalled the younger woman as someone I had seen on a fairly regular basis at the Fiesta Ballroom. In fact, I had spent a short time in her company in a bar in Letterkenny when we were both a lot younger and she had been, as far as I was aware, a nice girl from a decent family.

I think she recognised me too, though neither of us let on we knew each other. She had been caught shoplifting. Back then being convicted of shoplifting was a crime where the social disgrace far outweighed the actual offence. Around the same time in England there had been an outcry around the issue when an elderly woman, from the genteel classes, possibly suffering from absent mindedness, had committed suicide after feeling humiliated by a conviction for taking a paltry item out of a big London store without paying for it.

Some months before this I had been approached by a mother from Donegal whose son had stolen a cap for a car's petrol tank at a big store in the Waterside area of Derry. He too had been caught and was up in court. The woman was clearly at her wit's end: 'You know Mr McArt what the odd thing is – we own a motor repair business.. There are hundreds of them lying about here. Why did he bother stealing something he had absolutely no use for? I don't understand it at all.'

As she talked she disclosed his father had a serious drink problem, that he had been hospitalised on a number of occasions because of his alcoholism, the young lad was in trouble at school, and God knows what else was going on in his life. It didn't need a trained psychologist to know why he was acting like he was.

After these experiences I told the reporters to ignore someone appearing in court on a shoplifting charge but if they were second or habitual offenders forget it. Everyone was entitled to one chance. But that was it.

One rather odd incident was a woman who came to see me and on entering my office covered her face with a mantilla-type object. It was totally surreal, like a scene from an art-house movie. During the course of our conversation, I kept trying to get a good look at her face, but she sat sideways the entire time, and the only thing that moved while she was explaining that she had lifted the items by mistake was her mouth.

After she left, I went out to the reporters' room to ask if anyone had seen the woman with the mantilla and I got a blank look. I recall that woman to this day, but no one else does. I still think some believe I made her up.

On a personal level, I have lost good friends over court coverage. One in particular I used to go play football with several times a week. He would call for me or I would for him. I knew about his life, and he knew all about mine. There were few secrets between us. Then the shit in the fan.

His son had been found to have engaged in fraud and the father rang insisting the case not appear. As he was a professional man who knew exactly the position he was putting me in I tried to explain how I couldn't possibly put in a wee lad from the Creggan's case, someone up on a minor offence, while omitting his son's which was quite serious. I couldn't in conscience do that.

In the days that followed the rational old friend went out the window and the protective father came raging in. He was having none of it. Did I not understand how difficult all this was for him and his family? That his standing and good name and reputation would be dragged through the mud? He rang a number of influential people locally - including the proprietors - and got them to ring me, but by that stage he had made it impossible for me to drop it. I didn't go out of my way to give it prominence nor did I try to bury it but when it appeared it was the talk of the town.

That's way more than 20 years ago. He is dead now, but he never spoke to me again. If we did meet at a function, it was a curt nod.

One other man who had been close acted very similarly. His son was involved in a killing. What I found odd was that while he seemed to accept the law would take its course - he told people he knew the lad would do time - he objected to us, a newspaper, covering the trial. It was an odd view to take of an Editor's role and of the role of a newspaper in any community. Years too have passed since I had a conversation with him.

Of course, none of my stories top the one told to me during a press jaunt to Scotland by a well-known, colourful editor from the north's bible belt, Maurice O'Neill, of the Ballymena Guardian. Knowing the man concerned I have no doubt it was 100 percent true.

During a trip to Scotland as we were sitting at the bar Maurice told of one day getting a call from the wife of a local businessman asking if she could see him. Maurice painted a picture of a glamour kitten, married to a much older man who was regarded with suspicion as little more than a trophy wife if not an outright gold digger by the conservative circles – the church, the golf club, the yacht club – in which they moved.

When she rang asking to meet and would it be possible for him to stay on at the office for at least fifteen minutes after everyone had left, it really intrigued him, so he said no problem. Sure, enough the lady arrived looking a million dollars – a tanned, curvaceous blond, dressed expensively. It was, according to Maurice, no chore to sit and look at her.

And then out it came – why she wanted to see him alone. She explained she had been caught in a 'compromising position' which might be raised in a court case, and said he would only be too aware what the gossips locally would do to her reputation if details appeared in his publication. Even more importantly her husband didn't know, and she was particularly anxious that he not find out.

What could he, Maurice, do for her?

According to Maurice without another word she started unbuttoning her blouse in a very provocative way, clearly indicating she would make it worth his while to go along with her wishes.

'What did you do?' I asked Maurice.

'Don't be stupid, Pat.....I ran like hell...'

REFLECTIONS OF A REPORTER

The Journal newsroom was, like any newsroom, full of personalities, characters and, occasionally, chancers. But primarily, it was full of professional journalists. A former colleague Eamonn MacDermott made an observation in an article some time back about the 'old days' that I think sums it up very well.

Eamonn stated: 'One of the reasons it was such a professional workplace was that the journalists felt that they were treated as professionals and allowed to get on with the job they were doing.

'One thing that can be said about the Journal was that journalists were definitely not spoon fed. At the morning Editorial meetings, you could be told "you are doing the policing story". Now that very often would be the extent of the information you would be given. So, you would be expected firstly to know what the policing story was. If you didn't you were expected to find out.

'Secondly, then you were expected to know who to contact about that particular issue without being told. Then it was assumed you knew what to ask the various people you would be contacting.

'That trust in the journalist's ability meant that there was a team of first-class journalists who knew how to get a story. In case anyone thinks this is nothing unusual in other newsrooms reporters have been told, "phone so and so, ask them such and such and the like."

The Journal newsroom was also, again according to Eamonn, ahead of its time in that it was a family-friendly environment probably long before anyone had ever heard of the term.

I never thought of it like that.

I had trust in the staff not to take the piss and if they had genuine emergencies, I was more than willing to let them get on with it. As long as they cleared it with the Deputy Editor, Siobhan McEleney, there was no problem. In practice this meant that everyone had a lot of leeway when it came to those little emergencies like sick children or parents.

I described this over the years as a 'two-way street' approach – I looked after them, they looked after me. This attitude generally created an atmosphere where journalists felt they were not being watched and timed and so they reciprocated and didn't feel the need to time out or whatever.

In those days no journalist would ever have left before they were finished a story. Indeed, most journalists on Mondays and Thursdays would have stayed way after their hours until the paper was away. No one was timing them in in the morning and they did not feel the need to time out in the evening.

Eamonn MacDermott reflected that in later years – I had gone by this stage - when the powers-that-be introduced what was called 'five-over-seven' working and were warned this would create a factory mentality.

'And this is exactly what happened – people began to say "I have finished my shift and I am away home". You even had page make-up people leaving at 5.30 with a page half done, something that would never have happened in the old days.'

This is not to say that it was all sweetness and light in the office during my time. Not by a long shot. Due to the strength of character of many of the individuals, arguments and disagreements were frequent especially on a Monday or Thursday when the paper was being put out. While everyone who worked there knew that the shouting and cursing was due to the pressures of producing a paper and didn't mean anything, outsiders were not always so sure of what was going on.

I can state for a fact many a student in on work placement – I learned this in conversation with some of them years later - believed that a physical fight was imminent such was the level of shouting, not realising that as soon as the paper was gone everyone reverted back to type.

MacDermott wrote of this too: 'A lot of the atmosphere in the newsroom was due to the management style which was such that people felt free to argue their point quite vociferously. Obviously at the end of the day when a decision was made that was it, but you could argue with the Editor who rarely if ever pulled rank.'

And then there was the lucky Editor thing. Let me put this in context ... several former colleagues have made the same point to me on numerous occasions, usually when out on a social occasion, that I was what they called 'a very lucky Editor'.

It's a theme Eamonn really warmed to when citing one particular example: 'One Monday Siobhan was in charge while you were in Belfast or somewhere. Anyway, by about 3.30pm there was not even an idea of a lead story. We had scoured the news baskets and there wasn't anything that could have been remotely turned into a lead. Anyway, you landed back, and you were no sooner in the office when a phone call came with what was potentially a lead story. Shortly afterwards another story appeared and within about twenty minutes there were four stories available, any of them making a good strong lead. Jammy or what?'

I like to think of it as being a good newsman – not lucky - but sure who knows!

But, of course, when the cat's away the mice can play, to misquote the poet.

Being somewhat isolated in my ivory tower in the Editor's Office I only learned reporters had some guidelines of their own, unwritten rules - as it were - of the newsroom. One, in particular, that I was made aware of later was that if you were ringing John Hume for a comment, you did not start the conversation with 'how are you, John?' as he would tell you in great detail.

Another one was in the lead up to the Good Friday Agreement reporters rang the main parties every Monday and Thursday for an update. The unwritten rule here was that no reporter would have to ring the SDLP's Mark Durkan twice in one week as he was such a consummate master of minute detail it was too much for one individual to take. The will to live was severely tested.

Then there was Mary McLaughlin's Lenten swear box, which I and others refused to contribute to. It was just as well it was only for Lent as we – well, me in particular - would have been out a fortune. UTV's Mark McFadden, who began his career in the Journal, once wrote that I took swearing to 'an industrial level' so I would probably have needed a bank loan.

One of the annual highlights was the Christmas Party – note the capital letters!

This was no ordinary party; this was the event of the year. Whether it was because it took place in the office after the paper was put to bed so people were tired or whether some of us drank too much, it was often a case of checking the next day what had happened, who had said what to whom, and how many apologies would need to be forthcoming.

There were numerous funny incidents. Several folks recall two reporters going to physically fight one year over something said months earlier. Only problem was that the aggressor didn't notice his would-be opponent was already comatose on the floor due to too much alcohol.

On another occasion a reporter won a bottle of brandy in a raffle and that afternoon they were all, unbeknownst to me, sitting drinking brandy in their coffees. Thankfully nothing of major import occurred as we might not have been able to cover it.

That there was great camaraderie in the office was beyond question. I was aware that sometimes a reporter assigned a story might not be the reporter who handed in the copy. They covered for each other and stuck together in ways that were truly admirable. I held the view that as long as the copy was handed in, I wasn't particularly bothered looking for an explanation.

Another example I am aware of was when the journalists used to go out together for no other reason than to get drunk. After one of these spontaneous nights one of their female colleagues was getting a taxi home but not before the driver was subjected to an interrogation. 'What's your name? Who do you work for? Where do you live?' All done in order to protect the colleague to make sure she got home safely. The funniest thing was that the person doing the interrogation was usually too drunk to remember their own name, never mind that of the driver.

While my management style was probably a reflection of my own personality – I wasn't particularly fond of a confrontational style – I also owe some debt of gratitude to Frank McCarroll.

One day early in my editorship he came into the office and I noting the mess, the unfinished cups of coffee, the copy lying all over the place, started to apologise.

'Listen, Pat 'he said, interrupting me, 'I don't care what your desk looks like. As long as you keep producing good papers you can have that desk looking like a bomb site.'

And he had one piece of advice early in my career that I followed for the rest of my career.

Again, one day he came into the office, and I was in the middle of a heated argument on the phone with someone or other, probably something that had been in that day's paper. He sat patiently until I was finished and then asked: 'Pat, can I give you a bit of advice that might be useful for someone like you in that chair – don't go looking for trouble. It'll find you. All you'll do is be stressing yourself out over a lot of small stuff. Keep your energies for the big battles.'

He was a very wise man.

LOOKING IN THE DAILY MIRROR

The halcyon period of being an independent, family-owned operation which could have its own difficulties – a lot of friends whispering in the ears of various family members was often, as has already been alluded to, a source of irritation and annoyance in both the Editor and Editorial offices, but it also had upsides in terms of connection with community and the workforce – came to an end like a juggernaut juddering to a sudden halt. No one saw it coming.

Suddenly, everything that had previously been stable and well tied down started to sway about. It was a bit like a volcanic eruption for the staff, many of whom had joined the company on leaving school and had never worked anywhere else.

By and large it was a loyal staff in that the proprietors, prior to rumours they were selling up, had massive support within the building. It was openly acknowledged they tried to do the right thing, and they did care passionately about the paper and its role in society.

But all that came to an end when the paper was put up for sale in the mid-1990s.

This turned out to be a bitter period from which a lot of relationships have never been salvaged. It's probably fair to say that none of us involved came out of it smelling of roses, but I would contend that the way it was handled at the outset laid the seeds for what was to become a very acrimonious sale.

The Troubles had made the staff one big unit which despite individual personalities and characteristics had one goal – to get the Journal out on the street every Tuesday and every Friday. The uniqueness of that time and place had created an extraordinary situation, certainly one I had not come across before – or since. There was a real loyalty there, most of the staff being people who had worked with the Journal their entire lives. They didn't know anything else.

The problems began in early 1997 when staff started to hear whispers and rumours of the sale from outside sources. As Derry was a place with very little economic activity this was totally unsettling. A takeover would, many realised, have adverse consequences for them so they wanted to know what was going on. For those, and there were quite a number, with families on the verge of costly third-level education opportunities the loss of a job would have not only devastating effects on them personally but would affect their families as well. This was serious.

I felt I was between a rock and a hard place as I did know considerably more than what I was publicly admitting.

I had been at home shortly after Christmas in 1997 when I got a call from Bill Breslin, the General Manager of the Wholesale Newspaper Services who were the distributors of the Journal.

Bill, because of his massive contacts across the North, heard, to mix metaphors, the grass growing when it came to what was happening in the newspaper world. He knew Editors, reporters, newsagents, drivers and if Bill didn't know it, it wasn't worth knowing.

'Hey, McArt,' says he at the off, 'yous are for sale. It's definite this time.'

Some months earlier myself and himself had discussions on rumours floating about that Tony O'Reilly of the Independent Newspapers Group had made a bid but as we could not make that rumour stand up in any way, we forgot about it.

This was different.

Bill explained that Jim Campbell, who was Editor of the Northern edition of the Sunday World, had been at a party over the Christmas period in, of all places, California where he had met a number of Irish people. And, as coincidence would have it, one of them just happened to know the McCarroll family.

Whatever conversation transpired during that exchange Campbell, according to Bill, had no doubt whatsoever the paper was most definitely, no ifs or buts, on the market.

On returning to work I immediately approached Colm with what I had been told – without telling him the source of my information – and he told me it was bullshit. I was less than convinced by the response but in the absense of concrete evidence of any sale I had no reason to disbelieve him either.

All that changed dramatically months later when early one morning I got one of his famous 'have you got a minute?' calls asking me to come to his office. He was really excited.

This time he laid it out on the table. He hadn't, he claimed, lied to me the last time, just hadn't told me the truth. Which, in fairness to him, was not unreasonable. There were problems then within the family, some wanting to sell some wanting to hold on, but that had changed and now it was definitely for sale.

And then he dropped a real bombshell. There had been an offer from one potential buyer for £18.25m and it had been accepted by the family.

Why he was talking to me was that he was one of those who very much wanted to hold on to the paper and, surprise surprise, he was hoping to be the new owner.

I asked him how the hell was he going to do that?

His accountants, he explained, after doing the maths, had figured out a way for him to do so. The banks, I was told, were willing to invest, he would put in his share of the sale, and it was felt the annual revenue generated by the Journal would make the whole deal commercially viable.

He wanted me on board and he explained that it would not only be a good deal for us all but for me personally. From my understanding that morning it was all systems go.

I honestly don't know what happened after that, but it all exploded within days. It was clear there was a major falling out within the family, Colm was absent from the office and the recently appointed General Manager, Jean Long, became his representative at all meetings.

To say it rapidly became one unholy mess would be way too mild; it was a disaster of monumental proportions. The local radio station, Radio Foyle had regular stories about the upheaval. I was getting calls from just about every national newspaper and broadcast media. Someone, maybe more than one, was feeding stories that were doing the image of the paper no good.

Inside the building what had been a harmonious workplace was now a cesspit. There were those whose loyalty to the McCarroll family was unswerving, a loyalty based on their behaviour in the past. Others thought that bullshit, that these staff members were naïve in the extreme, that they were supporting those getting out with their millions whilst the dole office was the likely destination for many of them in the weeks and months ahead.

Initially, I tried to stay neutral but that was akin to attempting to swim without getting wet. It was impossible to stay on the sidelines. Like anyone with a brain I had zero problem with the McCarroll family selling the paper. It was their paper to sell and they had every right to do so. That was not the issue.

Where I was conflicted was them keeping staff in the dark. It was not, in my opinion, the way to treat people who had been loyal to the family over decades. The McCarrolls claimed that the sale conditions were extremely restrictive in what they could say or do. This was regarded with outright skepticism by quite a few who felt they deserved better, that a bit of decency in spelling out the basics of what was going on would not require any breach of the confidentiality clauses.

What was fuelling this outrage was that the people most affected, the staff, seemed to be the least well informed whilst numerous outsiders were up-to-speed on the latest twists and turns of the sale.

I was later to learn that some people in the circles in which the proprietors moved were not averse to divulging titbits of information they had gleaned from private conversations. Indeed, it was not uncommon to see little groups of staff gathered and animated conversation as the latest snippet of information heard overnight was digested.

What was galling was that these little snippets would often prove to be entirely true so whoever was getting the information had, seemingly, a well clued-in source. I found myself stuck in the middle of two factions with diametrically opposed views. As I said, I tried to stay well clear of it all but that stance lasted less than a couple of days.

The proprietors were telling the old staff, many of them there a lifetime, that nothing would change, that they would be looked after. The staff, like me, knew this was for the birds.

My road to Damascus moment was not long in coming. The NUJ members had a number of emergency, lengthy meetings which were seriously affecting production and I had participated in them. As Editor that was not out of place for me to do. But that all changed when Joe Martin, the Father of the Chapel for the GPMU print union, came to my office and asked me to come talk to his members who were then holding a meeting. The Editor officially meeting with print union members would be really crossing the Rubicon.

It was another of those defining moments in life, and I genuinely didn't know what to do. I asked Joe to give me ten minutes.

As I sat there, I thought: 'What do I do here? What side do I take?'

I knew if I went out to talk to the print staff my actions would be seen as unprecedented by the McCarrolls, that no other Editor had done so, that it was outside my responsibilities to be dealing with trade unions at a time like this. But these were people I had worked with, people who had supported me, who had helped me at every turn. To me they were my tribe, my people, the salt of the earth. I owed them.

For some reason the thought of my father came into my head. He had been a working man all of his days, and I remember him telling me of the many days he had to bend his will, to keep his mouth shut in the face of what he regarded as unfair treatment. That he had a family to feed meant his options to speak out were limited. For a proud and decent man this was often humiliating. He had no one to speak out for him or to stand with him.

I decided to cross the Rubicon.

I don't recall a lot of what I said other than there would be major changes coming down the track. It didn't need a crystal ball to see that. I also said that I didn't believe that their jobs were safe.

The newspaper industry, as I pointed out earlier in this book, was in the throes of massive change, the one industry hit more by hi-tech innovation than almost any other. Some of them knew nothing about computers, and little about the vast array of new news gathering techniques, equipment and platforms that were coming down the track. It was a tsunami that was unstoppable.

* * *

It all came to an end when on July 9, 1998, RTÉ News, confirming that 200 plus years of local ownership was no more, ran the following:

'Mirror buys Derry Journal Group for £21.5m...

DAVID MURPHY reports on a significant expansion of the British group's presence in the North. The Mirror Group yesterday significantly stepped up its presence in the North as it bought the Derry Journal and its three sister titles for £21.5m. cash.'

Reporter Eamonn MacDermott recalled this period of massive upheaval when stating that the staff had stayed loyal to each other and looked out for each other during the chaos of that period.

He went on: 'There was an issue that somebody kept feeding stories to Radio Foyle on the progress of the takeover. Then one of the owners accused you in public of leaking the stories prompting a reaction that could have led to a walkout of staff if the individual had not walked away.'

I can state categorically that I was not but that someone was, most definitely, leaking stories of the turmoil and in-fighting that was ongoing at that time to various media, particularly the BBC.

Every second or third day I would get a call, usually from the News Editor at Radio Foyle, Jim Lindsay, informing me of the latest and looking for a comment. I knew Jim well and knew him to be a decent sort but despite repeatedly telling him I couldn't comment on his latest piece of scandal dressed up as news the rumours all made their way onto the local airwaves. The only reason I was talking to him so often was to deny stories, not to plant them.

I, for the record, deeply resented being accused of being the source of those leaks. Anyone with a brain would have figured out they were making my life at that time a real misery, so it was far from my own personal interests to be leaking stories.

I'll leave Eamonn MacDermott's reflections to conclude this chapter: 'In those days the Journal was a big paper and acted like a big paper. We were sent all over the country to cover news. I was at the Assembly on the opening day. I covered the Patten report in Belfast and then the coverage following the Omagh bomb was second to none. All in all, the Journal Newsroom was a great place to work, to learn the trade as a journalist and to watch history in the making. That that is all gone now is to be regretted.'

'MONTY' ARRIVES

Prior to the sale we had any number of putative suitors, so no one knew what to expect when it finally happened. For a long time, it was thought the all-powerful Irish Independent Group, which had earlier paid a massive sum for the Belfast Telegraph, would be first out of the traps. Then there was talk of a Belfast-based grouping backed by a venture capital firm. As it turned out we got one of the most high profile figures in the British media as our new boss.

David Montgomery was the CEO of the Daily Mirror and said to be both a staunch unionist and a union-buster, a somewhat contradictory set of values. Born in Bangor, Co Down he had attended Queen's University where he studied history and politics and edited the student magazine The Gown.

In 1973 he joined the staff on the Daily Mirror. He became chief sub-editor in 1978. Two years later he moved over to the rival publication, The Sun

Montgomery was later editor of the News of the World from1985 to 1987. He then became director of News (UK) Limited owned by Rupert Murdoch's News Corporation. Between 1987 and 1991, Montgomery was Editor of the Today newspaper, again owned by Murdoch.

He was that rare animal – a journalist who crossed over to the business side of newspapers.

His Wikipedia entry states: 'Between 1992 and 1999 he served as chief executive of Mirror Group plc - publishers of the Daily Mirror and other national titles and a range of regional titles - following the death of its previous owner Robert Maxwell in 1991. During his tenure as Mirror Group CEO Montgomery oversaw a number of changes, including taking a stake in The Independent and its sister-paper The Independent on Sunday.'

David Montgomery was a controversial figure. He had earned the nickname Rommel, after the famous WW2 German general, from British journalists who were less than pleased that a former colleague had crossed over to 'the other side' in the unions versus management battles that were raging within the newspaper industry at that time. The battles were all about redundancies as new technologies were making old practices obsolete.

So, at the Journal the general consensus was this was a guy who would, probably, neither understand the ethos of the paper – and, being unionist, would probably have little sympathy with it – nor would he be sympathetic to staff.

He would be all out to cut jobs and increase profits. No wonder the perception of his imminent arrival as our new boss was not greeted with any enthusiasm. Dread would be the more apt word.

Anyway, the day arrived, and this big chauffeur driven car pulled into the Journal's narrow little car park. I presume there was some sort of greeting party but as I stayed in my office, I am not sure who exactly met him on his arrival. Eventually, however, he did make his way to me, and he was not what I expected at all.

He was the nearest thing to Rishi Sunak, the British Prime Minister, that one could see barring the fact that Montgomery was white. He was small, slight to the point of emaciation and somewhat owlish. But he definitely had that indefinable 'something'.

Instead of talking about cuts he talked about investing in new equipment and getting the building up to speed. He was only supposed to stay about ten minutes – he had a plane to catch in Belfast that afternoon – but he got so engrossed in the discussion he stayed closer to forty and then all but ran out of the office.

I can't say we became best friends but in the coming years I got to meet 'Monty' fairly frequently and I never saw the side of him that the British media did. He was unfailingly polite, always supportive and, unlike most journalists, obviously much more adept at business than we were.

I actually liked him and when some years later he became the first outsider to buy a major German newspaper a German reporter rang me up to ask my opinion of Monty. I told him I had zero problems with him, and that I couldn't speak for everyone but if he treated them the way he treated me they'd be grand.

It was only afterwards I thought how come the Germans had contacted me?

I presume it was Monty's PR people who must have read somewhere that I had nothing bad to say about him and dropped my contact details to a few media outlets.

Overall, I don't know how it would have panned out but had the Mirror stayed in ownership I think the Journal would have stayed the course so much better. There would have been, I would contend, less interference and more support. The Mirror had a national newspaper approach to the business, that spending money was not a problem as long as there was a return.

But, unfortunately, not too long after we got taken over the Mirror got taken over itself by the big provincial English newspaper conglomerate, Trinity Newspapers, and so we became part of the Trinity Mirror Group.

And it reverted to the growing ethos that I felt then was destroying regional newspapers – the relentless hunt for short-term advertising revenue even if it was to the long-term detriment of the paper.

The attitude reflected a near-contempt for the reading public; let's get the cash in.

As I have pointed out several times already, by this stage I could see the writing on the wall for people like me. Increasingly the power was shifting away from editorial to advertising, and it was the advertising manager who was calling the shots in terms of both pagination and, more importantly, key spots for advertising.

To explain this, in the Journal we had an 'understanding' between the editorial and advertising departments that the key news pages – that is, pages one, three, five, seven and nine – would be heavily dominated by editorial content and only key advertising would appear and would take up no more than about twenty-five per cent of the space.

That 'understanding' was now constantly undermined by advertising under constant pressure to sell, sell, sell, and to meet revenue targets that increased almost weekly. I came to the conclusion that some days the advertising was dominating the news pages, not the editorial. Indeed, it got so bad at the Journal I frequently complained that it had reached the stage if someone put in a classified advert, or an obituary notice, the advertising staff would promise them a free photo and a full write-up, guaranteed to appear in both the Tuesday and Friday editions.

As a reader I would have got pissed off with this and many did. The contempt I mentioned earlier manifested itself openly when the publishers began increasing the price of their products about every six months whilst cutting the pagination to such an extent there were days you could almost spit through the paper you'd be buying at the newsagent it was so thin. Why would any punter give up his/her hard-earned cash paying far more for far less?

It was but another nail in the coffin lid, which was hammered down by people within our industry, not by outsiders.

And I was only too aware that the whole ethos – and it was an ethos – was changing and I was becoming a dinosaur. I couldn't change. I didn't have that adaptability.

CIRCULATION CRITICAL, TERMINAL EVEN

My grandfather, Hugh McGhee, was, by all accounts, an avid reader. Every Friday he would get his papers – always more than one – and, according to my mother, would sit reading for hours on end the reports of councils and courts. He did his reading at the kitchen table in his home way high up in the hills of Drumkeen, outside Letterkenny, by the light of a Tilley lamp in a house that never was hooked up to electricity.

The newspapers were both his education and entertainment, and, of course, a ready source of material for conversation when neighbours met up. In an era long before television or social media newspapers were the source of information.

As a young boy I heard folks say he was a 'smart man' because he could talk about anything, that he read a lot, that he was always up to speed on the local issues not only in his community but in the county. The fact that he had only a basic national school education did not deflate that status of a learned man in any shape or form. Newspapers were his go-to source for all of this.

My father too was a newspaper man.

For the best part of forty years, he bought two papers daily - the Irish Press in the morning and the Evening Press later in the day. On Sunday without fail he bought the Sunday Press and the Sunday Independent and, years later when it became the new kid on the block, the Sunday World.

My mother, I heard on a few occasions, lamented the purchase of the latter because of its lurid headlines and considerable use of semi-clad females but back in the day it was different, stirring up the stale old newspapers which had reflected the politics of the Civil War – the Irish Press, DeValera's 'republican' paper, the Irish Independent, the paper of the 'west Brit Blueshirts' – and my dad, I think, found its difference appealing.

The influence of newspapers was everywhere. For instance, the aforementioned Justice Michael Larkin, during one of our many discussions on the way to various local courts, observed that newspapers were a vital part of democracy, that the old adage that justice must not only be done but be seen to be done was the vital cement which held the blocks of society together. A fair and accurate reporting of courts, which was a legal requirement under the laws of libel, was, he felt, an important part of giving people faith in the system.

And how seriously he took this was that if he looked around and saw there were no reporters in court, he often substantially increased the fine on the defendant.

I asked him why this was so.

'Because,' he explained, 'half the punishment for anyone appearing before the court is the opprobrium of their neighbours and friends. If their court case appears in the paper that's a deterrent because most people are ashamed to be in court. If there are no reporters and the case never appears in the paper, people breathe a sigh of relief thinking they have got away with it.'

Back then this was without question one hundred percent on the mark. In a deeply conservative society where adherence to the teaching of both religious and civil authority were benchmarks which often determined a family's standing in the community, having a black sheep – or a blackguard which was a word frequently used in old court reports – bringing shame on a household was not something dismissed lightly.

Indeed, it is hard to imagine today living in that kind of society where the laws and the rules were so rigorously applied, and rigid observance of them was expected of the Catholic community in places like Derry and Donegal. On several occasions in the early Sixties, according to my predecessor, Frank Curran, the Resident Magistrate in Derry, a man called Paddy Maxwell, was presented with a pair of white gloves. These were presented to mark the fact that not a single court case was on the list for that day's hearing.

Unfortunately, that was then, and this is now.

Today the newspaper industry, if not in terminal decline, is on the critical list. Just look across the pond and the figures are stark. Back in the 1990s The Sun newspaper – whether it meets the definition of a newspaper is debatable – regularly sold four million copies. It was so successful – it was making a million quid a week profit at one stage - it was said to be the financial platform that Rupert Murdoch used to go on to world media dominance.

The Daily Mirror was not far behind it at three million plus.

The latest figures I could get from Google is that The Sun now sells just over one point two million copies whilst the Mirror is down to just over half a million.

Closer to home The Irish News is now selling somewhere in the region of 25,000 copies daily and the News Letter just under 8,000.

It is hard to believe that back in the day the Derry Journal sold more in a small, concentrated area than the Irish News does today. And the fact that the readership per copy, considering the size of families back then, was probably way higher than it is today meant the Journal's reach and influence was way more powerful than any comparison with now.

But as an old newspaperman with ink still in his veins the prediction made in April this year by CEO of Mediahuis, Peter Vandermeersch that his group – which publishes Ireland's largest selling newspapers, including the Irish Independent, Sunday Independent, Belfast Telegraph – that within ten years print versions of newspapers will be no more, that all news will be online, is heartbreaking.

In my opinion newspapers were unique, informative and what's more provided free lessons on how to write properly. It was a form of education for readers. Somehow, I don't see an electronic medium, where grammar and spelling and mangled language are commonplace, fulfilling that role any time soon.

And while electronic media is global there are few protections and laws governing that are global, hence all kinds of propaganda, hate speech, libels and the rest can easily dominate. By way of contrast, laws governing newspapers are rigorous. The libel laws in this country, North and South, are amongst the strictest in the world. While not perfect, that is still a great protection for the average reader.

A STORY OF TWO PATHS

Throughout our childhood, we never missed nine o'clock mass on a Sunday morning.

All seven us scrubbed up in our Sunday best, shoes shining like a mirror and the white shirts on us boys crisper than a packet of Tayto. Stepping out the front door of our house on the Church Lane in Letterkenny we would join the throng heading to St Eunan's Cathedral. And just to make sure we observed our religious duties later the same day we had to go at six o'clock to Benediction.

It might sound ridiculous now but the Catholic church's grip on society was not unlike the Taliban in Afghanistan. Its reach was massive, its psychological handcuffs dictating the mores of how we lived our lives. If you wanted a job as a teacher, you had to be seen to be not only a mass-goer but a communicant. The same applied for those wishing to be trainee nurses or those seeking a job in the civil service. If you had fallen foul of the parish priest at any stage, you hadn't a hope.

In many rural parishes even the places of entertainment such as the local dance hall were run by the Catholic Church. The irony of that was not lost on many of our great writers over the years. There was strict segregation of the sexes, legendary stories of priests coming directly to couples on the floor instructing them not to be dancing so closely.

My top story is where this kind of thing crossed over into total farce.

In the border village of Muff, a local who was involved in the community came to me about an entirely different issue but before leaving he remarked that 'you have to hear this one'.

He proceeded to tell the story that a local parish priest at the time was approached by some parents about holding dances for the boys and the girls as there wasn't much by way of amusement or entertainment for young teens in the area. He willingly agreed. Known to be an arch conservative in matters of interaction between the sexes, it amazed those who had approached him how quickly he had agreed to their request.

One of the parishioners wanted to make sure they had not misunderstood him so decided to get it absolutely 100 per cent clear:

'Are you sure Father you have no problem agreeing to a disco for the boys and girls of this parish in the parish hall?'

'Not at all', he replied, 'it'll be grand. How about Tuesday night for the girls, and Thursday night for the boys?'

I have never been able to confirm if this story is true, not some kind of urban myth, but I was told by several that it definitely happened.

This is the kind of community I grew up in. But then so did Stephen Blake. But he chose a very different life.

I hadn't seen Stephen for about thirty years when I was told he would like to meet me in our hometown of Letterkenny. He wanted to have a chat. Knowing his story, I was intrigued and readily agreed to meet up.

I soon observed that unlike myself Stephen was clearly used to his own company. In his compact little house on the outskirts of the town there were no photos of family, no paintings or souvenirs. It was neat and tidy, more functional than homely.

There were other give-away signs, too, of the solitary life – no toys strewn around, no clothes draped over armchairs, the television was tuned to a horse racing channel with the sound turned down, there is an ashtray with quite a few cigarette butts and while we talk he frequently gets up to walk around as if he's in a cage.

'Do you mind me walking about…I have to do this,' he says, without explaining why he has to do it.

As he prowled around, I started to ponder about the vagaries of life, about the paths we take and what led us to taking those paths. Like literally hundreds if not thousands of others Stephen and myself both grew up in Letterkenny in the 1960s in council estates. Both our families were, on the surface at least, similar. My father had emigrated as a young man to Scotland as had Stephen's. We were Catholics, members of large families. We both went to the same Christian Brothers primary school.

My road took me into journalism, Stephen's took him into the IRA.

Years of solitary confinement in English jails explained the constant walking in a confined space. Those years have left a very definite imprint on him. All his conversations are peppered with stories of what happened in various gaols, about the beatings, the riots, IRA men who are no longer with us. It's clearly all living still in his head. The day before our meeting he'd been off visiting Johnny Walker, one of the Birmingham Six, who spent eighteen years in jail for a crime he didn't commit.

As I sit drinking his coffee and he's smoking one cigarette after another he starts telling stories.

One guy he remembers from his first IRA camp, shot dead a policeman in England. An Irish-American, this guy came all the way from the States to join the IRA. His conversation is littered with casual references to people like this.

When asked directly he struggles to explain how it all came to pass.

He doesn't really have an explanation, so he starts telling a story: 'Ours wasn't a republican house; my mother didn't want to know about things like that. She had no time for it at all. Her father was in the Old IRA but then so was half the country at that time so that was no big deal. I don't think I got any influence in that direction at all. None that I am aware of anyway.'

It was a tough childhood, with a lot of tragedy and trauma along the way.

Suddenly he sits down and there's almost a stream of consciousness as he speaks, like I am not there: 'My abiding memory of my childhood was the day my wee brother, Gabriel, was killed. He was three. It was a Friday and myself and my mother were sitting eating poundies (mashed potatoes) and butter at the table by the front window. It's as clear today as a photograph. I remember seeing a car and hearing a bang and seeing a wee body go up in the air. We all went running out. There were a whole lot of wee boys in our street at the time and my mother started shouting, "Where's Gabriel?"…. but sure it was Gabriel who was knocked down…..'

Where was your father in all this?

'My father died three months after Gabriel. He was killed in Scotland. It's not a happy story. I don't think he was up to much. He was a migrant worker – a good enough worker, by all accounts – but he was a drinker and a womaniser, and he didn't give my mother a penny. I suppose you could say he was a waster. I'll tell you the kind of man he was…

'Our Gabriel didn't die until late on Friday evening and when he was contacted my father was said to have to rung Hughie McGovern (the undertaker) to make sure he was dead. That was the type of man he was. He was making sure he wasn't going to waste the money for drink coming home for nothing.'

Why did he do that?

'He didn't want to come home. That's what I take out of it. He was living, or so I was told, with a woman in Scotland so it might have interrupted whatever he had going on there. Anyway, he did come home, and we didn't see eye to eye. I was 12 then and I suppose I was trying to be a man.

'I remember one morning coming down the stairs - it could have been some days after Gabriel's funeral – and saw him sitting in a chair in the front room all suited and booted and ready to go drinking or whatever and he said to me:

"How are you?" I said not as well as you. And I said, "Know the best thing you can do for us? Fuck off down that road".... and he did. That was the last time I saw him. Three months later he was dead.'

All these years later Stephen doesn't know the details of how his father died. When I expressed surprise at his lack of curiosity, he became defensive.

'We were never told the circumstances surrounding his death. Some of my relatives went over to Scotland to bring the remains home but it was never talked about. '

Stephen pulls no punches either on life back then; there are no rose-coloured spectacles of a happy Irish childhood.

'It was grim. It was a daily battle to survive, just to have enough to eat. I robbed. I robbed rings around me. There were days there was literally nothing to eat in our house and sometimes even in winter there was nothing to heat the house. I became a sort of messenger boy around this time. I don't think my older siblings would do it; they had too much pride to do what I did. My mother used to send me with notes to various people in the family and I would come back with the likes of tea and bread.

'Looking back now I'm sure people hated to see me coming. I was begging. Always begging. And if I could lift some coal or turf or whatever came my way I did. And when I would come home with stuff I shouldn't have, my mother would ask, 'Where did you get that?' and I would tell her to mind her own business. She knew what was going on, but we were desperate, so she turned a blind eye to it.

'Oddly enough, in later years when I brought this up, she didn't want to know about it, didn't want to talk about it.'

When the Troubles broke out in Derry in 1969 the young Blake approached well-known Letterkenny republican, Pat Dawson, and was eventually inducted into the IRA.

I wondered if he considered the consequences, that what he was doing was actually very dangerous. The lifespan of an IRA volunteer was estimated to be, at most, seven years as by that stage they would either be dead or in jail.

'I don't think I did. I think I was trying to be John Wayne. Dawson's house was the clearing house where people from Strabane or Derry came when they wanted out of the North for a while. I was ordered to take them to houses in Glencolmcille or Gweedore or wherever. Or take someone injured up to the hospital. It was small stuff. I suppose they were watching to see how I would turn out.'

From that he went on his first IRA training camp at a farm just outside Letterkenny.

'Me and another local were the two Letterkenny men there. And there was the American who later shot the cop in England. There were a couple of boys from Derry there at the time too. The training officer was a Cork man. He died just a couple of months back. He was a good man. We were taught how to use a Lee Enfield rifle, a Thompson submachine gun and how to make bombs.'

And then I got the only answer I was going to get regarding him joining the IRA: 'You keep asking the same question - you want to know why I joined? The answer is I didn't give a fuck. The more danger I was in the better; I liked it, the adrenalin I suppose. I was only happy when I was in a corner. I think it was the robbing I had done to survive as a wee fella was at the root of it. That had given me a real adrenalin rush, so this was adrenalin on steroids.'

I have often reflected on this conversation. The paths we choose – is it nature or nurture? Fate or personal choice?

In my years in journalism I have come across so many families divided beyond healing because of what went on in our country. I have lived through a time when I heard a father telling a court that a son who took part in a killing was 'no longer my son'. The events in the North were not just about the violence but the rending apart of families, communities and society.

It's hard to see even at this stage how real healing can take place unless there is some sort of reconciliation process where all truths can be heard.

THEY ARE ALL GONE NOW....

They are all dead now, the big players during my time as Editor of the Derry Journal – Hume, McGuinness, Daly. They led big lives, lives I'm sure they never envisaged running around, certainly in Hume and McGuinness's case, the back streets of Derry.

Sometimes when I reflect on my conversations with them, I am not sure they were ever totally comfortable in the glare of the spotlight. I often thought them a bit like the swan, in that the calmness seen on the surface was not necessarily what was going on underneath. Both Daly and McGuinness, in particular, were far from extroverts.

Over the years my relationships with them all grew more comfortable and trusting even if it was not always a warm embrace. I knew I could tell them things that would go no further and vice versa. Many were the stories I learned off-the-record during those conversations, things that most people can guess were usually far more interesting than what was said on the record.

Hume, in particular, could tell you what half of the leading politicians across Europe and US were saying and doing behind the scenes. He was not relying on newspapers or gossip for this as he was talking to them directly himself.

A blind man on a galloping horse couldn't have missed the fact they were all under constant pressure, living lives on the front line in a place traumatised by violence, and where they were expected to lead from the front in times of crisis.

Little wonder they developed various defence mechanisms for coping. Hume was happiest getting away from it all down in Greencastle where he could sit at his house near the sea and do his crosswords and go for a stroll along the Moville to Greencastle pathway. I met him there a couple of times.

McGuinness' idea of heaven was to get away to some remote part of Donegal and go fishing or walking his dog. I am not sure what Eddie Daly did with his down time, but I presume his religious calling helped.

While McGuinness had his stresses during the peace process, bringing the Republican Movement on to the path of peace – and that was serious stress – Hume was getting venomous abuse from an unexpected source, the Dublin 4 media cohort.

It would be remiss of me not to put on the record that some of the so-called journalism, if one could call it that, was an absolute disgrace and that the columnists and editors responsible should be hanging their heads in shame to this day. Much of the coverage was both nasty and vindictive, akin to watching pygmies trying to bring down a giant. It was also arrogance, people who knew next to nothing about what was going on behind the scenes in the North trying to tell a man who did, that he was wrong and they, from the safety of their computer desks in Dublin, were right.

For instance, when the famous Hume-Adams talks were outed by Eamonn McCann – Eamonn, by total fluke, saw Adams coming out of Hume's home at West End Park – all hell broke loose. Hume was pilloried in most quarters but particularly in the Sunday Independent.

Much of it was downright vitriol. Hume, it was suggested, was giving oxygen to terrorists, that a man of his stature talking to them was giving legitimacy to their campaign of violence.

The reality was that nothing could have been further from the truth. He had got involved in the talks at the invitation of Fr. Alex Reid, a priest based at the Clonard Monastery in Belfast who knew Adams and believed that if he could get the two main leaders of the nationalist community to talk, they could, maybe, find common ground which could lead to a pathway to peace. It was peace Hume valued most of all, and that was his objective in talking to the president of Sinn Fein.

I asked Hume about it all on numerous occasions and he openly admitted that it was tough, that he was hurt by the abuse, that he didn't like being targeted in this way, but he felt he had to keep the talks going. I suggested that some of the abuse was libellous – one article in particular in the Sunday Independent was absolutely scurrilous - but he said that if he went down the legal road that, while he might get personal vindication not only would he get side-tracked personally but that the talks would probably end. And he felt that while he could well win a legal battle it would be a pyrrhic victory, that in conscience he had to keep going, because he had some innate intuition that he was getting somewhere in the talks.

'And how are they going?' I asked him.

'Well, Adams tells me,' he replied, 'that if the guy up the street is happy, he's happy. And, apparently, the guy up the street is happy.'

He didn't need to spell out that the 'guy up the street' was Martin McGuinness. Take from that what you will in regard to the significance of McGuinness's role right across the Republican Movement.

One story that follows directly on from this was when Albert Reynolds came to Derry and called down to the Journal offices. He was no longer Taoiseach, but we got talking and he mentioned the Hume-Adams talks. I said I had actually seen the document.

'That's more than I ever fucking did,' retorted Albert, claiming that Hume had hung not only himself but his government out to dry when telling the media before heading off to some big shindig in the States that he had given Albert the final document.

'I had to lie to the media people, telling them we were studying it, that we were needing more detail before we could respond. It was rubbish. I was buying time. I didn't see it then and I haven't seen it since.'

Perhaps I should put it on the record that Hume showed me the Hume-Adams document late one Thursday night as I came out of the Delacroix, the pub next door to the Journal. I used to go for a few pints of Guinness with the proprietor, Frank McCarroll Snr, after putting the paper to bed as this marked the end of the working week. It was our weekly safety valve.

This particular night the last person I expected to come across was Hume who had been waiting for me. He wanted copies of the Journal straight off the printing press as he was heading off to Belfast Airport for an early morning flight.

We strolled over to the Journal building, into the press room and with the printing presses making an awful racket in the background I heard him say - 'Here, have a look at this. Some of you people [media] are saying it doesn't exist. Well, you can say you have seen it.'

I did see it. But I have to own up, that's about all I did. Not only was it the end of the week, I was very tired after about a fourteen-hour day and I had drunk several pints of Guinness at that stage. What I will say is a lot of it, if my vague recollections are anyway accurate, was contained in later documents issued prior to the all-Ireland vote on the Good Friday Agreement.

But, keeping in mind the importance to history of those talks – they were the basis of the IRA ceasefire and the Good Friday Agreement – the fact that I saw the Hume-Adams document and don't remember it other than in the vaguest of terms doesn't go down as my finest hour.

The years went on and as I never kept a diary or took notes, I don't remember exact dates, but I do recall meeting Hume fairly regularly. On one particular occasion he was not in great form telling me he was tired and concerned about his health.

What had alarmed him to a degree was he had just returned from America where he had met a consultant psychologist at a dinner in California. And he warned me that what he learned had implications for me too.

This was the story in John's words that I recall pretty much verbatim: 'I went to this dinner, and I was sat beside this man who I got talking to and I learned that he was a senior medical consultant, a psychologist. So, I said to him that I was feeling tired, that sometimes I had trouble focusing and that sometimes I couldn't remember people and places I should have known no bother.

'He said to me: 'What do you do, Mr Hume?' and I told him I was a politician in Northern Ireland. And he warned me I needed to be very careful of my long-term psychological health. I asked him why and he explained it like this.

'He said – 'Mr Hume when a carpenter comes into work on a Monday morning and is told he has to make a table and four chairs before Friday he knows what he has to do, and the time allotted to do it. So, he gets to work and when he finishes on the Friday, he switches off his brain and thinks about what he's going to do for the weekend – play golf, go hunting, whatever.

'But there are two groups of people who, in particular, can't do this – politicians and journalists. There is no switching off on a Friday evening, no equivalent of the table and four chairs sitting finished. And that's the problem – there are no Friday evenings for politicians or journalists. The brain is like a muscle that needs rest, or it will wear out eventually. And there is the danger for people like you. You can't switch off.'

I asked John if he was worried about it and he replied: 'Jeez, Pat, look at how many politicians got Alzheimer's – Harold Wilson, Margaret Thatcher, Jack Lynch. You should be concerned too.'

Considering how dementia was to later destroy that mind, that intellect that was the size of a planet, it was prophetic in a way. In the years that were to follow his intelligence never declined but his ability to focus most certainly did. Sometimes when he came to my office he would be talking and then he would go silent for five minutes, stare at nothing in particular and, believe me, it made for some very awkward moments. I am not good with silence.

During these periods I often saw him light one cigarette, take a couple of drags and then snuff it out, only to repeat the exact same process minutes later. Come to think of it, he must have spent a small fortune on fags.

Bishop Daly was another man with health problems in that he suffered badly from kidney disease. He had a kidney removed at one stage and frequently needed renal treatment. A diffident person sometimes in public, away from the glare of the spotlight he could be a very different person. Like Hume, he loved telling stories of people he met along the way, and the more eccentric they were the more he liked it. And he had a wealth of stories to tell, quite a few of them he put in print on retirement in his book 'Hi Mister, are you a Priest?'

Not only had Eddie Daly one of the biggest dioceses on the island of Ireland and, particularly at that time, one of the most demanding, he also had the added difficulties that it straddled the Border. One diocese, two jurisdictions.

A large part of north Donegal was included so as bishop he needed to be up to speed on two different political approaches, two education systems – the Catholic church was front and centre back then in education – and, as he believed in keeping in touch with not only his priests but his various congregations, he would try to ensure annual pastoral visits to every parish. It was a punishing schedule for anyone in top physical shape but for a person who had his health problems it must have been heavy going.

We were in regular contact as he kept all his press statements for Mondays and Thursdays so that they would appear in that week's editions of the Journal.

One day he rang up saying he had a statement on abortion so myself and himself got into a real debate about it. I found his attitude to be more liberal than most of his brother bishops, basically a position that while he totally opposed it, he could understand why women in certain circumstances would think they had no other choice. His stance was much more about compassion than condemnation.

I asked him if he would say publicly what he had just said to me and in response he told me to take a running jump to myself, but in language considerably stronger than that. He was a genuinely good man for whom I had a lot of respect.

In contrast with Hume, Martin McGuinness and I got off on the right foot almost from the start. Just a few months after taking over as Editor he had been in the office where he learned something personal about a member of another party, something that would have been seriously advantageous to Sinn Fein.

When I was told about it, I approached Martin and said to him that while I understood that in politics all is fair game, but I would appreciate it if he didn't disclose it publicly, that it would be an embarrassment for me, and it would cause me problems with the person concerned.

He assured me that he wouldn't, and he never did. He kept his word.

Another incident I recall was when one of our reporters made a real mess of a court report involving a couple of well-known republicans. I was informed their lawyer was going to ask for a mistrial using the erroneous report as the basis. I rang Martin and explained the situation, that it was a genuine error on the part of the young reporter, that it would again cause real trouble for both the paper and the young lad if a re-trial was ordered by the court. I added that I had no doubt it wouldn't change the outcome of the verdict either.

Martin listened, and then said, 'Forget about it. I'll sort that out.' He did.

And one final thing worth putting on the record.

Over the years I had been a sort of go-to person when it came to Martin. I did numerous broadcast interviews, particularly with the BBC, when attempts were being made to analyse what was going on within the Republican Movement. It was obvious McGuinness was the key player there.

I recall the day it was publicly announced that McGuinness was going to be the Sinn Fein lead, the new Michael Collins as it were, in official negotiations with the British. I did a lengthy interview for BBC radio news following the announcement. They wanted to know what sort of person he was, what his likely position on key issues were etc. I chatted away, thinking nothing of it.

About a fortnight later I got a cheque for something like sixty five quid. As the usual fee was half that, I wondered why it was double. When I checked I was told that, very unusually, they had used nearly all of the interview – more than six minutes – so the fee was doubled.

What I took from that was the Brit media really were interested in knowing who they were dealing with.

At that time Adams was considered the political lead in Sinn Fein, Martin the warrior chief. It was shades of DeValera and Collins from back in the day. He hadn't done a lot of media work, mainly the silent partner in the background. Now he was emerging from the shadows as a key political figure.

So, now here we were years later in the run up to a much anticipated IRA ceasefire and I was getting daily calls from all over the place. Would they? Wouldn't they?

As the Derry Journal was the first paper on the island of Ireland to predict a ceasefire was coming down the track everyone wanted to know what was happening? What did I know? What did our reporters know?

The republicans still negotiating hard with the British government - the old maxim that nothing was agreed until everything was agreed was very much in play in the final days - wanted to give nothing away, so it was a closely guarded secret if they were going to go for an historic deal. And if they were, they were going to milk it for all it was worth. They knew an end to the Irish conflict was eagerly awaited right across the globe; the ending of the world's longest running urban conflict was big news.

Martin came down on this particular Thursday with two other Sinn Fein members. As they were leaving, I asked more in cheek than any real expectation of an answer, 'And when is this ceasefire going to be announced?' and he replied with a big smile 'God only knows' and went on out.

About two minutes later my office door opened and Martin stood there and said quietly: 'If I was you, I wouldn't take next Wednesday off.'

I think he did it this way, so that the other two wouldn't know that he had told me.

To this day I have reason to believe I was the only journalist who knew when the IRA was going to announce the 'cessation of all military activities'.

And to this day I feel honoured that he trusted me enough to tell me that, and to trust that I would not leak it.

I think of all the people I met during my time as Editor he was the one who made the longest journey. He started out a warrior, talked openly about 'the cutting edge of the IRA' to force political change and then fought with the same tenacity for peace. For me, whether you agree or disagree with his path in life, Martin McGuinness was true to his beliefs in war, and he was true to them in peace. It was the same person who pursued both.

I don't think we will ever see the likes of these people again.

EPILOGUE
Never do a Shankly...

As I write this we are coming towards the end of 2023, and, as mentioned in the first chapter, much has changed in Derry since I arrived more than 40 years ago. The positives are out there. The vibe in the city is brilliant. There is a real energy. The checkpoints and the oppressive air are gone, replaced by an almost cosmopolitan lifestyle. There are even pleasure boats on the Foyle. On summer days it's a stirring sight to see people sitting and dining in pop-up restaurants and food-stalls along the quays. There is a real continental feel to it all.

Even in winter it's great to see folks strolling around enjoying an alfresco experience, walking the bridges, meeting old friends, even listening to the accents of the many tourists who were once up there in terms of rarity with hen's teeth. The old joke about the BBC programme where the first prize was a week's holiday in Derry and the second prize was two weeks is long gone. Derry is buzzing with the craic, with the talent of its people.

But investment in the city from the Belfast-centric Stormont-led parliament and civil service can only be described as pathetic. Job creation projects are thin on the ground as potential investors are still, seemingly, steered east of the Bann on almost every occasion. A clear indicator of the economic disparity is the simple fact that disposable income in the North West is way below that in the east.

So, to quote an old political party slogan, 'A lot done – a lot more to do.'

On a personal level leaving the Journal was a momentous decision for me. And I was determined that should I leave I would cut my ties totally. The legendary Bill Shankly was asked to leave Liverpool's Anfield training ground in the mid-1970s as the new boss, Bob Paisley, had reached the stage where he felt his authority was being undermined by Shankly's daily presence at the club. Shankly had decided months earlier to leave but then found he couldn't go.

I was determined not to do a Shankly.

I made a point of not going near the office and not contacting old colleagues when I retired. I thought a clean break best for everyone. I had seen too many people become nuisances.

Strangely enough, it helped that a few years earlier a former SDLP mayor of Derry, John Kerr had, albeit inadvertently, given me a sound bit of advice.

One Thursday night in the Catholic Club after putting the paper to bed I got talking to John and he told me that when he lost his seat on Derry City Council his phone, which was never off his ear, suddenly went silent. Even people he had regarded as personal friends no longer rang him. You could see he was genuinely hurt by that, and also at a loss. His life, he explained, that had been helter-skelter busy with calls from constituents, council workers, officials from various departments, the media etc was now filled by the loud tick-tock of a clock in a home where he sat with nothing to do.

I took note of that, and I prepared for that scenario.

I was very aware that many of the people who were never off the phone or calling into the office were not calling to see me, Pat McArt, they were calling in to talk to the Editor of the Derry Journal. I had never confused the two. I always knew who my real friends were.

So, I faced into retirement at 52 with a reality check, but that's not to say it was easy. No way. At the start it was really difficult. Put it like this, it's really hard to get used to walking pace in a life where you have been sprinting full on.

For about the first six months it was a rarity that my nightly dreams were not related to the Derry Journal – I was back in the Editor's Chair, Hume was on the phone from America, McGuinness and Mitchel McLaughlin were bending my ear about something. And ghosts of people who were dead – Domhnall MacDermott and Siobhan McEleney in particular – haunted me. I would wake up in the morning heartbroken when the renewed realisation hit me that they were long gone. That it was all gone.

The drama of it all had dominated my life for so long I hadn't realised I was addicted to it. But you do adjust – eventually – to a new way of living. I started doing bits of work here and there. I went back, as told in an earlier chapter, part time to the Journal. I also started doing work for other people, a newspaper column here a column there. And, eventually, I even started teaching creative writing courses that I thoroughly enjoyed.

I also started walking a lot. That really was therapeutic. Come rain, hail or shine myself and Murphy, our black Labrador, would go strolling for a couple of hours. That dog and I bonded big time. I cried my eyes out when he died.

For the first time in 25 years, I started losing weight instead of putting it on. Having clothes that fitted for a change was also really nice, though that experience of weight loss was relatively short-lived.

On one of those walking days – this would be long after I retired – I ran into Martin McGuinness down at Inch Level. He was Deputy First Minister by this stage. We stood chatting for about twenty minutes, and he told of how he was finding the arrogance of the DUP tough going, that they were behaving like people who owned 'the hotel' and that nationalists were, they seemed to think, like the staff who could be told what to do.

It was an unusual analogy but perfectly apt for what was apparently going on at that particular time. It was the last time I was to meet him face-to-face.

I met Hume too one blisteringly hot summer's day when I stopped off at a small shop in the village of Muff. The short version of a long story is my wife went into the shop, got talking to John, told him I was outside and out he came. And I realised within seconds he hadn't a clue who I was.

I tried to find common ground, even mentioned a few people we both knew well but he looked at me blankly. His dementia had taken over totally. And that I found sad beyond measure.

At the outset I was at pains to point out that this was a memoir not an autobiography. It's a memoir in that I really only concentrate on various events, but there's one story that is autobiographical that, perhaps, shaped my life more than any other. I think it worth recounting in this last chapter.

It's about my father.

My father's mother died when he was two. His father remarried but, true to form, the stepmother-stepson relationship was far from good. But it shaped him in a way that we, his children, benefited greatly from. He made sure we came first, that he always put us ahead of himself. His life was living proof of this.

The story goes that he got out of a sick bed on a wet Monday morning in the winter of 1947 to go work for the ESB digging holes as the rural electrification scheme was rolled out. He was, he told me as an old man, as 'weak as water' from a bad dose of the flu but as work was scarce and he had a young family, needs must. What was on offer was casual daily employment - at the end of the day, the foreman decided who was let go and who was kept on – so it was vital he got through it.

And that day, he suggested, a bit of a miracle occurred.

My dad who had spent all weekend in his sick bed got to where the ESB gang was gathered and was sent to dig six feet holes for the huge electricity poles. This was at the far end of a field where farming activity would be rare, so he was expecting the worst – that the ground would be rock hard.As men around him faltered in the icy, hard ground, he had no bother. He was able to finish the job in half the time.

But that wasn't the full story.

Until the day he died he contended that someone must have dug the same patch weeks earlier as despite sweating profusely and feeling really unwell he finished his section first. I can only presume that as a boy brought up on a farm, he knew this was fact, that it was truth - something had made it easy for him.

Of course, the outcome of it all was the foreman, on seeing his work finished in record quick time, was duly impressed and he was taken on for the rest of the week, and eventually given full-time employment. That day changed his life and changed ours.

Had he not got this job he would have become like thousands of other Donegal men of that era, an emigrant worker going over and back to Scotland and England to work on the sites, the roads or the farms. And there is every likelihood we as a family would have eventually emigrated. Many did. Maybe I could have ended up as Editor of the Glasgow Herald or the Yorkshire Post? Who knows.

In the middle of 2022, the Derry Journal celebrated its 250th anniversary. I was invited to contribute an article.

I'll end with the last paragraph I wrote in that contribution as I can't think of anything that sums up my views better.

'I suppose looking back I would have to say the Troubles did totally overshadow my entire Editorship. And I am not going to gloss over it and say they were the good old days – they weren't. They were tough, they were demanding, and many were the nights I lay awake into the wee small hours worrying.

'But here's the thing: Would I do it all again?

'Absolutely, in a heartbeat...'